INDIANAPOLIS

HEARTLAND HISTORY

Jon K. Lauck, *editor*

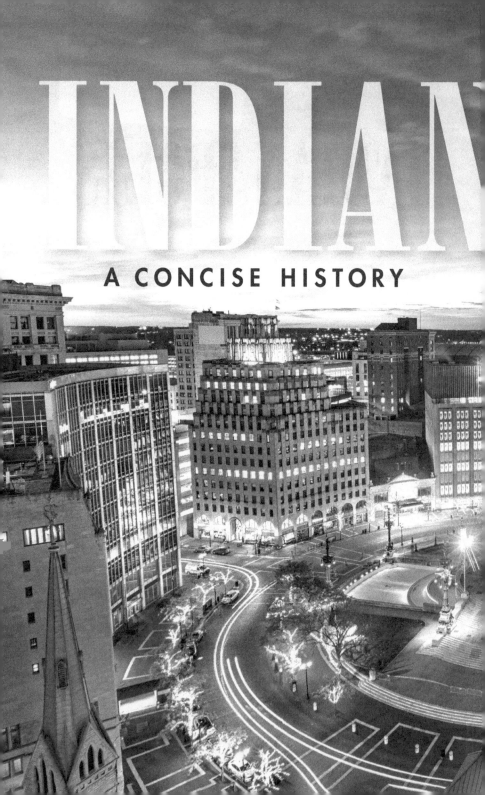

INDIAN

A CONCISE HISTORY

APOLIS

Jon C. Teaford

Indiana University Press

This book is a publication of

INDIANA UNIVERSITY PRESS
Office of Scholarly Publishing
Herman B Wells Library 350
1320 East 10th Street
Bloomington, Indiana 47405 USA

iupress.org

Manufactured in the United States of America

First Printing 2024

Library of Congress Cataloging-in-Publication Data

Names: Teaford, Jon C., author.
Title: Indianapolis : a concise history / Jon C. Teaford.
Description: Bloomington, Indiana : Indiana University Press, [2024] | Series:
    Heartland history | Includes bibliographical references and index.
Identifiers: LCCN 2023033686 (print) | LCCN 2023033687 (ebook) | ISBN 9780253068958
    (hdbk.) | ISBN 9780253069238 (pbk.) | ISBN 9780253068972 (web pdf)
Subjects: LCSH: Indianapolis (Ind.)—History. | BISAC: HISTORY /
    United States / State & Local / Midwest (IA, IL, IN, KS, MI, MN,
    MO, ND, NE, OH, SD, WI) | HISTORY / Social History
Classification: LCC F534.I357 T43 2024 (print) | LCC F534.
    I357 (ebook) | DDC 977.2/52—dc23/eng/20231025
LC record available at https://lccn.loc.gov/2023033686
LC ebook record available at https://lccn.loc.gov/2023033687

CONTENTS

INDIANAPOLIS

The Marmon Wasp driven by Ray Harroun, the first
winner of the Indianapolis 500, 1911.

Introduction

Indianapolis is two hundred years old. In 1824, Indiana's state government moved to Indianapolis, so 2024 marks the two-hundredth anniversary of Indianapolis's role as the political center of Hoosierdom. Over those two hundred years, the city has also become the state's unequaled urban hub. As its name denotes, Indianapolis is without rival as Indiana's city.

The city's sesquicentennial in 1971 saw the publication of Edward Leary's *Indianapolis: The Story of a City*, a volume that ably commemorated the city's achievements. Now, more than a half century later, the time is right for an updated history—one that carries the story into the twenty-first century and illustrates themes that have emerged as increasingly important in the past fifty-plus years. The following work seeks to fill the gaps as well as reiterate the highlights of the city's earlier development. During the last decades of the twentieth century, the city achieved new recognition as a model of urban revitalization, and its Unigov scheme of government attracted national attention. Its heritage of racial division assumed new significance in an age of school desegregation through busing and persistent tension between African Americans and the police. Historic preservation has transformed Indianapolis neighborhoods deemed irredeemable in 1971. Moreover, it has fostered a heightened interest in the city's heritage. From the perspective of the postindustrial and deindustrialized twenty-first century, Indianapolis's once-dominant manufacturing past can now be seen as a transient factor in the city's development and not as an essential element of urban prosperity.

The city and the world have changed, and Indianapolis merits a new history chronicling its past in light of that change. Indianapolis has been a city in the making for two hundred years. Its story includes achievements and setbacks. There have been embarrassing interludes as well as proud moments. The following pages recount the challenging two-century odyssey of the Hoosier capital.

1

A State Capital Is Born
1820–1850

The state of Indiana gave birth to Indianapolis. State agents chose the site of the city, the state legislature named it, and state-commissioned surveyors drafted its street plan and laid it out; the state owned the land on which it was located and sold the original town lots, the proceeds of which were to pay for state government buildings. Indianapolis was a public enterprise, created by and for the state government. And prior to the late 1840s, this public enterprise was the foundation and mainstay of the Hoosier capital. During the first quarter century of Indianapolis's history, there was a private sector of stores, taverns, churches, artisans, and small-scale mills, but state government was the reason for the community's existence and sustained the struggling town through challenging times. Private entrepreneurs made little headway in advancing the community and profited only from the town's status as a seat of government. Indianapolis was the state capital but little else.

THE FOUNDING

In 1816 Congress admitted Indiana to the union and authorized the donation of four square miles of the federal government's public land as the site for a capital city. The new state could select this donated tract anywhere it chose. At the time, the nascent state legislature met at the small village of Corydon in far southern Indiana only fifteen miles north of the Ohio River. Most of

Indiana's white population resided adjacent to the Ohio in the state's southern extremity, near the western border settlement of Vincennes, or in the east along the Whitewater valley. The center of the state remained the domain of Native Americans and still off-limits to white settlement. In 1818, however, in the Treaty of St. Mary's, the Native Americans relinquished ownership of a vast expanse of central Indiana that became known as the New Purchase. With this area open to settlers of European ancestry, the state now had the opportunity to establish a new capital in the center of the state. Such a site would supposedly offer equal accessibility to future legislators from all the state's outlying regions and not favor the north, south, east, or west. Indiana was not unique in seeking a centrally located capital. Ohio chose Columbus as its seat of government because of its central location, and the same would be true of Springfield in Illinois and Jefferson City in Missouri. Legislators preferred a capital in the heart of the state, equidistant from the northern and southern boundaries and the state lines on the east and west.

Consequently, Indiana lawmakers were determined to abandon Corydon and avail themselves of the federal government's generosity by selecting a four-square-mile tract in the New Purchase. On January 11, 1820, the legislature appointed a commission to choose a capital site. The commissioners were to meet at William Conner's trading post on the White River in central Indiana in the coming spring and explore the region for an optimal location for the state's new city. On June 7, 1820, the commissioners reported that they had selected a site where Fall Creek entered the White River. They had sought a tract along the White River because they believed it was navigable and thus would provide water access to the capital. Since water transportation was the best mode of travel in frontier Indiana, the commissioners believed a river site would be the most convenient to lawmakers arriving for legislative sessions and would enhance the commercial prospects of the new settlement. Commissioner Joseph Bartholomew explained that the chosen tract was "as nearly central as any that could be selected; and perhaps, unite[d] as many natural advantages as any spot of ground in the western country." It was "a high, dry, rich and well timbered piece of ground" and abounded "with the most excellent and durable streams for mills and other machinery of every description."[1]

In January 1821 the legislature confirmed the commissioners' site selection and chose the name of the new city. Some legislators believed that a Native American name was most appropriate for the capital of a state named for Indians. Marston Clark argued in favor of naming the city Tecumseh, an ironic choice since the great Native American chief had devoted his life to preventing whites from settling in the West and creating states such as Indiana. The legislature rejected his proposal, but Clark suggested other Native American names that also failed to win favor. Another lawmaker offered the name Suwarrow as an option, which seemed of indigenous origin, but that won no support. Jeremiah Sullivan proposed Indianapolis, the name of the state combined with the Greek word for city. That met with an outburst of laughter from the assembled lawmakers, but eventually the legislators adopted Sullivan's proposed appellation with little opposition. Sullivan later recalled that the principal reason for adopting the name was that combining *Indiana* with *polis* would "indicate to the world the locality of the town."[2] The English translation, Indiana City, would have achieved the same end, yet by opting for the Greek *polis*, the lawmakers invoked the imprimatur of the glorious classical past. Indiana's capital was not to be a run-of-the-mill settlement; instead, it was to be a capital worthy of modern-day solons.

Not everyone, however, was impressed by the name. A Vincennes newspaper that had preferred Tecumseh lambasted the choice. "One of the most ludicrous acts . . . of the sojourners at Corydon, was their naming of the new seat of state government," editorialized the newspaper. "Such a name, kind readers, you would never find by searching from Dan to Beersheba; nor in all the libraries, museums, and patent offices in the world." It was "like nothing in heaven, nor on earth, nor in the waters under the earth." According to the Vincennes newspaper, it was "not a name for man, woman, or child; for empire, city, mountain or morass; for bird, beast, fish nor creeping thing; and nothing mortal or immortal could have thought of it except the wise men . . . who were congregated at Corydon."[3] No amount of invective or purple prose would convince the legislature to change its mind. The capital would bear the name of Indianapolis.

On the same day it approved the name, the legislature chose three commissioners to lay out the town site. Only one of the three, Christopher Harrison, actually took charge of the task, and he appointed Alexander Ralston and Elias Fordham as surveyors of the new town. Ralston seems to have been responsible for the plan drafted for the capital. He was a native of Scotland who had assisted Pierre L'Enfant in laying out Washington, DC, and his plan for Indianapolis reflected the influence of L'Enfant.

Ralston laid out a mile square in the center of the four-square-mile donation tract. Henceforth, the core area of Indianapolis would be known as Mile Square, as Ralston's original plat would become synonymous with the city's future downtown. In 1821, however, Ralston felt one square mile was sufficient to accommodate the entire capital city for decades to come. The remaining land in the donation tract was set aside for out-lots intended primarily for agriculture. His Mile Square consisted of a grid of one hundred square blocks with twelve lots in each block. As in L'Enfant's Washington, DC, diagonal avenues would overlay the grid and converge on four central blocks surrounding a circle that was intended as the site of the governor's house. Two blocks west of the circle was the site for a future state capitol building, and two blocks to the east of the circle was the lot dedicated to the county courthouse. Ralston envisioned a city of broad boulevards with each street ninety feet wide. An exception was Washington Street, a grand thoroughfare 120 feet in width.

Ralston's plan was not the commonplace grid of streets typical of so many towns in the emerging Midwest. A few years earlier, surveyors had laid out Ohio's new capital of Columbus in such a grid; its plan was indistinguishable from that of every other country town in Ohio, Indiana, or Illinois. In contrast,

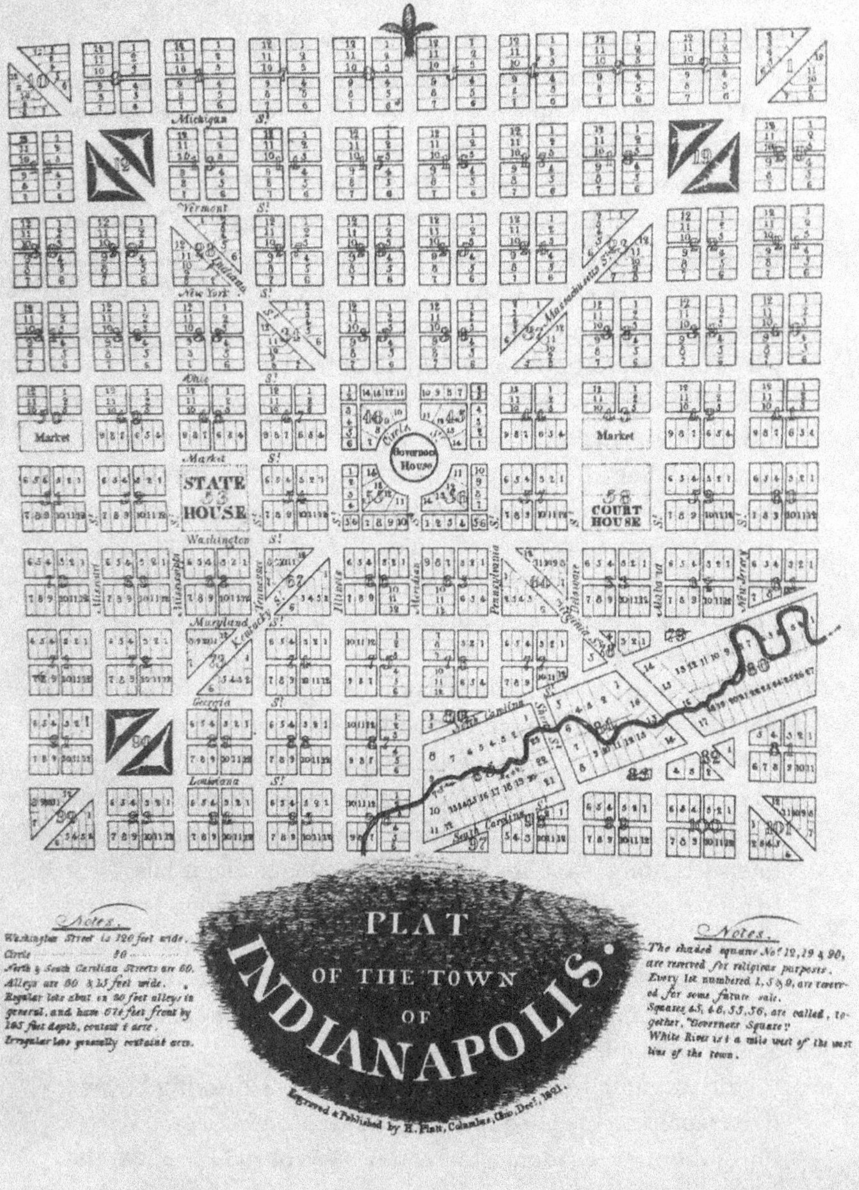
PLAT
OF THE TOWN
OF
INDIANAPOLIS.
Michigan St.
Vermont St.
New York St.
Ohio St.
Market St.
Washington St.
Maryland St.
Georgia St.
Louisiana St.
Market
STATE 53 HOUSE
Governors House
Circle St.
58 COURT HOUSE
Indiana
Massachusetts St.
Kentucky
Illinois
Meridian
Pennsylvania
Delaware
Alabama
New Jersey
Missouri
Mississippi
Tennessee
Virginia
South Carolina St.
Notes.
Washington Street is 120 feet wide.
Circle 80
North & South Carolina Streets are 60.
Notes.
The shaded squares No.s 12, 19 & 90, are reserved for religious purposes.
Every lot numbered 1, 5 & 9, are reserved for some future sale.
Squares 45, 46, 55, 56, are called, together, "Governors Square."
line of the town.

The Ralston plan

Indianapolis's plan emphasized the new settlement's role as a capital city. The diagonals focused attention on the central circle and the proposed home of the state's chief executive. Washington Street was broad enough to accommodate grand patriotic processions, and the statehouse and county courthouse were sited equidistant from the circle, creating a carefully balanced city of governmental symmetry. Indianapolis was not to be a town like every other town. Its very form announced it was a capital city. Indianapolis's circle was the center of a community with grand aspirations to be the hub of the state.

Reality deviated markedly from Ralston's paper plan. The town site was densely forested, with as yet few settlers and no public buildings. There was little reason for a thoroughfare 120 feet wide. In the uncongested wilderness, forests and morasses were more serious obstacles than throngs of people or masses of traffic. Realizing that his plan was largely a dream for the future, Ralston observed that Indianapolis "would be a beautiful city if it was ever built."[4]

Optimistic Hoosiers, like Ralston, recognized the future possibilities of the settlement and gathered in October 1821 to bid on the town lots the state was offering for sale. The state sold 314 lots, requiring buyers to pay one-fifth of the purchase price at the time of the sale and the remainder in equal installments over the four succeeding years. The proceeds from this and later sales were to fund the construction of the state's public buildings. Prospective owners who failed to meet the terms of sale forfeited 169 of the purchased lots. Investors were gambling on the future of the town, but it appeared that many were overconfident about their ability to complete their transactions.

With an ambitious plan and surveyed lots drawing buyers, Indianapolis seemed to be on the path to becoming a capital worthy of the state. Gradually there were signs of civilization in the wilderness settlement. In February 1822 the federal government designated Indianapolis as a post office, with Samuel Henderson as the first postmaster. Simultaneous with the opening of the post office was the printing of the first local newspaper. George

Smith and Nathaniel Bolton founded the *Gazette*, which at first appeared only an average of once every two weeks. In 1823 a second newspaper, the *Western Censor and Emigrants' Guide*, published its first issue. Yet the frontier town remained remote from the rest of the world. In 1823 an editorial complained that most of the eastern mail came via Lawrenceburg on the Ohio River and "arrive[d] here but once in two weeks."[5] News from the outside world was slow in arriving, but after some delay, Indianapolis pioneers could keep apprised of what was happening by reading the pages of the *Gazette* and the *Western Censor*.

Some Indianapolis residents were also enjoying the civilizing influence of religion. As early as 1821, local Methodists relied on circuit riders to lead their worship. Baptists organized a congregation in 1822. A year later the Presbyterians formally established a church. Though the nascent settlement was remote from centers of culture and learning, it clearly was not God forsaken.

There were other diversions for those seeking more profane amusement. In December 1823 Indianapolis pioneers were able to attend their community's first theatrical performance. Among those present was early settler Calvin Fletcher, who recorded in his diary that "the performers were Mr. And Mrs. Smith purporting to be directly from the New York theaters." Though "they both were not less than 50 years of age," they performed a farce called the "Jealous Lovers." They returned for an encore appearance in June 1824 and received a scathing welcome from the *Western Censor*. The newspaper claimed that their "performances were treated with so much contempt and ridicule last winter" and contended that encouragement of the Smiths "would evince a want of taste and discrimination in our citizens." The editor of the rival *Gazette* was less critical, noting that at the December exhibition, the sixty-year-old Mrs. Smith not only acted but also sang "The Star-Spangled Banner" and danced "a hornpipe, blindfolded, amongst eggs."[6]

Though the Smiths' performances may have proved disappointing, Indianapolis residents had reason to rejoice. In January 1824 the state legislature made the final decision to move the capital to Indianapolis. The 1824 session would be the last one in Corydon. The period of planning and preparation was over. Henceforth, the state's government would be based in Indianapolis.

Beginning in 1825, the legislature met in Indianapolis's Marion County Courthouse. In 1821 the legislature had designated Indianapolis as the seat of the newly created Marion County. Work on a courthouse was completed in the fall of 1824—just in time to accommodate state officials and lawmakers. The new combination courthouse/statehouse was a two-story brick structure measuring fifty feet by fifty feet. Members of the state house of representatives met in the first-floor courtroom, and the senate was assigned a room upstairs. The clerk of the Indiana Supreme Court used a thirteen-by-thirteen-foot office on the second floor, and the secretary of state's office was in a similar space immediately below. For the following ten years, Indiana had no capitol building and did not benefit from Alexander Ralston's grand vision of a statehouse two blocks west of the circle. Instead, the state government of Indiana was stuffed into a small, undistinguished county courthouse and lacked a home of its own.

State officials moved to Indianapolis in the fall of 1824 prior to the first legislative session to be held in the settlement. Indiana's lawmakers authorized the state treasurer, Samuel Merrill, to auction off "all the chairs, tables, and other furniture belonging to the state" that could not "be advantageously removed to Indianapolis." Having done this, in November, Merrill and the state printer, along with their families, embarked on the journey to the new capital. According to Merrill, "four four-horse wagons and one or two saddle horses formed the means of conveyance for the two families . . . and for a printing press and the state treasury of silver in strong wooden boxes." Given the remote location of the new seat of government and the primitive condition of roads, it was an arduous trek. "The journey of about one hundred sixty miles occupied two weeks," Merrill recorded. "One day the wagons accomplished but two miles, passages through the woods having to be cut on account of the impassable character of the road." Twenty years later Merrill reminisced about the journey, commenting on the poor, muddy state of the primitive pathways leading to Indianapolis. He claimed that he experienced "the depth and width of mud-holes that cannot well be conceived."[7]

Lawmakers arriving in Indianapolis in January 1825 for the settlement's first legislative session must have shared Merrill's concern about the inaccessibility of the centrally located seat of government. Given the capital's remote location, the majority of the state's residents were cut off from what the legislators were doing. A Lawrenceburg newspaper complained, "[It will] be impossible to have any information from the legislature before the middle of next week, nine days from the commencement of the session! (We can have information from the City of Washington in 11 days, which is more than five times the distance to Indianapolis.)" The newspaper accused Indiana's lawmakers of "wanting to have a place unconnected with the stir and bustle of the world . . . where they might vote as they pleased, and no person know anything about it." Supporting its argument that the state solons sought a wooded retreat away from public scrutiny, the Lawrenceburg journal quoted the poet William Cowper: "Oh, for a lodge in some vast wilderness! / Some boundless contiguity of shade."[8]

By 1825 Indianapolis was established as the seat of the state's government. The legislature was meeting there, and state officials had taken up their duties in the new capital. Yet in the minds of some Hoosiers, it was "a lodge in some vast wilderness" characterized by a "boundless contiguity of shade." Though a geographer might argue it was in the dead center of the state, in reality Indianapolis was at the northern edge of settlement and difficult to reach from more heavily populated areas. For too many observers, it seemed to be in the middle of nowhere.

THE FRONTIER VILLAGE

Over the following two decades, the capital settlement attracted additional residents and became a more acceptable seat of government. Yet it did not assume a preeminent position among the state's towns and cities. The condition of roads improved, but accessibility remained a problem. In an age of water transportation, Indianapolis suffered a definite disadvantage and was unable to equal New Albany on the Ohio River, let alone the fast-growing midwestern river cities of Cincinnati or Saint Louis. Despite its name it was not a polis, a city. Instead, from the 1820s through the early 1840s, it remained basically a frontier village.

The Indiana Gazetteer or Topographical Dictionary compiled by John Scott described the young capital in 1826. "It is supposed that this place now contains about 800 inhabitants," reported the *Gazetteer*. It was the site of "7 stores, 4 taverns, 1 clock and watch-maker, several cabinet-makers, carpenters, saddlers, hatters, shoe-makers, tailors, brick and stone masons, plasterers, chair-makers, wheel-wright etc." Completing the list were "2 printing offices, a post office, a library, a sund[a]y school, a bible society, and a masonic lodge—3 clergymen, 3 physicians, and several lawyers."[9]

In 1827 a local newspaper further described the town, which it claimed had "about 1,000 souls." It recorded "25 brick, 60 frame, and about 80 hewn log houses and cabins in town," as well as a Presbyterian church with "upwards of 30 members," a Baptist church of thirty-six members, and a Methodist congregation of ninety-three persons. With boosterish pride, it further claimed: "There are weekly schools in which some of the teachers would not discredit their calling in any part of the Union, and the same may be said of some of the members of each of the learned professions."[10] The community was no longer a wilderness, but there still were more than three times as many log cabins as brick dwellings, as well as an array of small businesses typical of a frontier village.

Indiana's lawmakers continued to invest in the young settlement. In 1827 the legislature appropriated money for the construction of a supreme court clerk's office adjacent to the county courthouse. It was a modest one-story brick structure containing two rooms; one was an office and the other a depository for records. More important, the lawmakers approved $4,000 for the construction of a governor's house on the circle as envisioned in Ralston's plan. As completed, the yellow-brick mansion was about fifty feet square with two floors plus a basement and attic. It was an imposing structure for the frontier capital, yet no governor chose to live in it. Instead, at times it housed a variety of state officers, including those of the Indiana Supreme Court, and was used for occasional public events such as governors' inaugural balls. It gradually deteriorated, and by midcentury tramps occupied the deserted structure. In 1851 a local newspaper deplored the "present and shabby condition" of the Governor's Circle, which had become "an 'eyesore' to our city," and urged the demolition of "the present dilapidated building."[11] It was demolished six years later, ending the thirty-year life of a governor's mansion never occupied by a governor.

A more pressing concern for those dedicated to the community's advancement was the lack of a water link to the outside world. During high-water seasons, flatboats and keelboats plied the White River as far as Indianapolis. By the late 1820s, however, the steamboat was coming to dominate the inland waterways of the United States. If Indianapolis was to advance as a city, it needed to be accessible to steamboat traffic. In 1828 a steamboat from Louisville advanced up the White River to within fourteen miles of Spencer, Indiana, and an optimistic Indianapolis editor expressed his belief that steamboats could make it to the capital when the White River was "well filled with water."[12] Eager to demonstrate the commercial potential of the capital, aspiring politician and promoter Noah Noble offered a $200 reward to the first steamboat captain who brought his vessel to Indianapolis. In April 1831 the steamboat *General Robert Hanna* made the ascent, unleashing a wave of rejoicing among Indianapolis's previously landlocked citizenry. Jubilant area residents lined the waterway cheering the vessel's triumphal voyage. A local editor proclaimed, "No event is recollected, since the first settlement of the town, which produced a higher excitement than . . . the arrival of this steamboat."[13] Recognizing the importance of the occasion, a local company of artillery paraded to the boat and fired a salute.

At a public meeting, a committee of citizens was appointed "to make arrangements to demonstrate . . . the high gratification" that was "felt by all who feel interested in our commercial and agricultural prosperity." The committee adopted a resolution stating that the boat's successful ascent "should be viewed . . . as a proud triumph, and as a fair and unanswerable demonstration of the fact that our beautiful river is susceptible of safe navigation for steam vessels of a much larger class than was anticipated by the most sanguine."[14] In recognition of the achievement, the committee invited the owners and officers of the steamboat to a public dinner.

Celebrating its success in conquering the White River, the *General Robert Hanna* took Indianapolis residents on two excursions up the river. On one occasion the vessel struck an overhanging limb that knocked down the boat's pilot house and chimneys. Some of the frightened passengers abandoned ship, jumping overboard into the river. Two days after its arrival, the *General Robert Hanna* departed on its ill-fated return voyage. It ran aground in the shallow river and remained stranded on a bar for six weeks.

Given its sad fate, the *General Robert Hanna* marked the end, rather than the beginning, of Indianapolis's history as a steamboat port. Boosters of the young capital had to accept the fact that the White River was insufficient as an artery of commerce. The grounding of the *General Robert Hanna* was a fair and unanswerable demonstration that the White River was not susceptible of safe navigation for steam vessels.

By the time of the steamboat's arrival, Indianapolis was ten years old. During its first decade, the settlement had attracted about one thousand residents and had the churches, stores, and local artisans and professionals typical of a midwestern county seat. As the meeting place of the state legislature, it did have a special distinction. Yet after a decade, the community's record of achievement was mixed. It was a capital without a capitol building, it was the site of a governor's mansion never occupied by a governor, and it was located on a purportedly navigable river that no steamboat could successfully navigate.

During the remainder of the 1830s, the frontier village enjoyed some advances and suffered some additional failures. It continued to seek better access to the outside world and develop a commercial as well as a governmental future. Unfortunately for local boosters, it did not prove an unconditional success and did not emerge as one of the leading cities of the fast-developing Midwest.

Not only were local leaders attempting to improve the community's transportation fortunes, they were also seeking to establish a manufacturing base. As early as 1827, an Indianapolis newspaper urged the community to produce more of the goods consumed by the town's populace. It estimated that "at least $10,000 annually" was "paid by citizens of Indianapolis for flour, whiskey, tobacco, gun-powder, spun cotton, hats and linseed oil, imported from abroad." The newspaper advocated for the creation of local industries applying steam power to rectify this outflow of cash. "Let the united efforts of our citizens provide for the erection of machinery," the paper editorialized. This "would not only relieve us from excessive drains of money but afford employment to the industrious of almost every age and capacity."[15]

The legislature responded to such entreaties and in 1828 granted a charter of incorporation to the Steam Mill Company, which was to operate a grist mill, a sawmill, and a woolen mill. Investors were slow to purchase the company stock. Construction did not begin on the factory complex until 1831. By the end of that year, the company had completed a sawmill on the west side of the White River and a five-story structure for the flour and woolen operations. The steam machinery arrived from Cincinnati by wagon, which, according to one early historian, was "a feat but little less in magnitude than hauling Pittsburg over the Alleghanies" in the early 1830s.[16]

The enterprise soon proved to be unprofitable. It was too big for a small, isolated community such as Indianapolis. It supplied the local market but also was designed to produce a large surplus, for which there were no buyers. Transportation was again the problem. The company could not ship its output inexpensively to out-of-town consumers. It could manufacture, but it did not have an economically feasible market for its manufactures.

Thus, Indianapolis residents were again reminded of the disadvantages of their inland location. Cincinnati was developing as a manufacturing hub for the West. Located on the Ohio River, it could cheaply supply the vast and increasingly populous Ohio and Mississippi valleys. Large-scale manufacturing simply was not feasible for a community that could not deliver its output at a reasonable price. Given the realities of its location, Indianapolis seemed destined to attract only small-scale shops and mills serving the local market. In 1835 the Steam Mill Company ceased operation and attempted to sell its machinery, much of which ended up as scrap iron. According to a later chronicler, "the vast building [was] left as a haunt for idle boys on rainy days, who played cards in the saw pit and [was] taken for an extemporaneous brothel and hiding place for thieves and their plunder."[17]

Meanwhile, there were some signs of advancement in the frontier village. In 1832 Indianapolis established its first municipal government. Until that time the capital was an unincorporated place governed by county and township officers. In accordance with a law recently enacted by the state legislature, the community submitted to the county board of commissioners a petition signed by at least two-thirds of the capital's legal voters asking for incorporation. The commissioners granted Indianapolis the status of an incorporated town to be governed by five trustees. Following their election, the first board of trustees chose Samuel Henderson, the former postmaster, as their president. Moreover, they adopted a general ordinance defining offenses and penalties. A malefactor who flew a kite, discharged a gun, or ran a horse within the town would suffer a fine of at least one dollar, though not more than three dollars. The trustees also penalized those who left firewood on Washington Street for more than twelve hours, as well as anyone who erected a stovepipe within two inches of woodwork. Equally heinous was riding a horse or operating a vehicle on the sidewalk, presenting a show without obtaining a license, or the unlicensed sale of less than a quart of whiskey.

The new town government also established regulations for the public market. During the summer of 1832, local citizens erected the community's first market house immediately north of the courthouse. The town ordinance specified the market would open at daybreak on Wednesdays and Saturdays and remain open for two hours on each of these days. The town's market master was authorized to confiscate and destroy any food he deemed unwholesome, ensure honest weights and measures, and seize any articles of fraudulently represented weight.

By 1832, then, the newly constituted town government was imposing order and some degree of honesty on the frontier village. If the trustees had their way, Indianapolis would not be the Wild West. It would be a community with a regulated, law-abiding citizenry worthy of a capital city.

In the mid-1830s, the state legislature was finally rectifying one of the most notable shortcomings of Indiana's seat of government. On January 26, 1832, the lawmakers approved a plan submitted by New York City architects Ithiel Town and Andrew J. Davis for a state capitol building. Town and Davis were two of the nation's most distinguished architects, and they were responsible for the design of public buildings throughout much of the nation, including the North Carolina state capitol and the United States Customs House in New York City. The legislature was, then, relying on respected experts in the field. It took three years to complete the building, but in December 1835, it was ready for occupancy. The new statehouse was approximately one hundred feet wide and two hundred feet long, with a footprint about eight times the size of the courthouse in which the legislature had previously met. It was modeled after the Greek Parthenon but was topped by a small dome. One early commentator reported that "it was proudly regarded by the people of the State as a monument of taste and munificence."[18] Some later observers were

Woodcut view of the Indiana statehouse, 1835

more critical, focusing especially on the inappropriateness of a Roman dome imposed on top of a Greek temple. One wrote of "the preposterous little dome" and argued that "the incongruous, contemptible dome should have condemned . . . [the building] utterly."[19] In his 1884 history of Indianapolis, Berry Sulgrove remarked that "the style was the Doric of the Parthenon, spoiled by a contemptible little dome about as suitable in that place as an army cap on the Apollo Belvedere."[20]

The building also suffered from poor construction materials, which resulted in its rapid decay. The exterior walls were brick and wood lath covered in stucco to resemble sandstone. According to Sulgrove, the stucco "looked well till frost and thaw, damp and heat began to make it peel off, and then it looked worse than a beggar's rags."[21] The foundation was of soft blue limestone that also decayed when exposed to Indiana's climate. An early historian of the city noted in 1857 that it had "rapidly gone to decay" and "at present [was] a disgrace to the State."[22] In 1870 it was quite frankly described as "disgusting."[23]

Once ensconced in their new Greek temple, Indiana's legislators enacted a scheme to boost the hopes of Indianapolis's citizenry. In 1836 the lawmakers approved the Internal Improvements System, an ambitious program for the construction of roads, railroads, and canals. One key element of the scheme was the Central Canal, a manmade waterway that was designed to run from the Wabash and Erie Canal in northern Indiana through Indianapolis and terminate in Evansville on the Ohio River. It was intended to provide the water link deemed so necessary to the advancement of the capital city. If completed, it would provide Indianapolis with a navigable water route from Toledo on Lake Erie and make the capital accessible by water to the great Ohio and Mississippi valleys. The Central Canal seemed a much-needed answer to the town's problems, as it promised a cure for Indianapolis's landlocked ills. News of the legislature's action "was hailed with delight by the citizens." According to one account, "Congratulations [were] every where extended, bonfires were built, rockets fired, and the town illuminated."[24]

Unfortunately, the state of Indiana could not afford the grand scheme. In the late 1830s, an economic depression blighted the hopes of speculators and investors throughout the nation. The state of Indiana suffered bankruptcy and had to retrench. That meant abandonment of the Central Canal project. Work had begun on the waterway, but when the state called a halt to construction, it had completed only nine miles linking Indianapolis to the small village of Broad Ripple to the north. At the close of the 1830s, Indianapolis was no closer to achieving water access than when the *General Robert Hanna* ran aground at the beginning of the decade.

The federal census of 1840 testified to Indianapolis's relative insignificance as an urban place. Indiana's capital had a population of 2,692. By comparison, the largest midwestern city, Cincinnati, was home to 46,338 people, and Saint Louis could boast of 16,469 residents. Ohio's capital of Columbus was more than twice as populous as Indianapolis, as were the Ohio cities of Cleveland and Dayton. In Indiana both New Albany and Madison outranked the capital city and seemed to enjoy better prospects for future greatness than Indianapolis. They were on the great Ohio River waterway and thus linked to Pittsburgh on the east and New Orleans on the south and west.

During the 1830s the National Road reached Indianapolis, relieving some of the town's isolation. Built westward from Cumberland, Maryland, it was the finest overland route in the trans-Appalachian region. The wagons traversing the National Road, however, could not match the steamboats on the Ohio and Mississippi Rivers as modes of transport. Nor could the road match the canal systems facilitating the movement of goods through Ohio. The Hoosier capital was on a main east–west overland thoroughfare, but the river and canal networks remained the greatest arteries of commerce in the West. Sadly, Indianapolis's abbreviated canal provided access only to Broad Ripple and not New Orleans.

Though the Hoosier capital did not seem a promising place to achieve fame or fortune, one future celebrity began an eight-year sojourn in Indianapolis after settling there in 1839. Henry Ward Beecher, who later became the nation's most famous preacher, took charge of the Second Presbyterian Church and laid the foundations for his distinguished career. Like his sister, the novelist Harriet Beecher Stowe, Beecher was a foe of slavery; he delivered an antislavery sermon in 1843, stirring ire among some Hoosiers who despised the abolitionists. Following two antislavery sermons three years later, a number of members withdrew from Beecher's congregation. Indianapolis might suffer from commercial isolation, but it could not escape the political rancor that was dividing the nation.

In the winter of 1843–1844, Beecher delivered a series of discourses on morality that were published as *Lectures to Young Men, on Various Important Subjects*. He inveighed against idleness, dishonesty, gambling, and "the strange woman."[25] When dealing with the latter subject, he refused to follow the example of more timid clergymen who were fearful of speaking of sexual licentiousness and vice. No sin escaped the eloquent Beecher's withering condemnation. His *Lectures* earned him a national reputation, a remarkable feat for someone in far-removed Indianapolis.

Benefiting from his new recognition, the preacher left Indianapolis for a pastorate in Brooklyn, where he would become one of the most widely known men in the nation. It was possible for the frontier village of Indianapolis to be a launching pad to fame, but once someone had achieved distinction, the capital carved out of the wilderness could not hold those who were ambitious. Remembering the Indianapolis of the early 1840s, Beecher later wrote, "With the exception of two or three streets there were no ways along which could not be seen the original stumps of the forest. I bumped against them in a buggy too often not to be assured of the fact."[26] Beecher's wife, Emma Bullard Beecher, was certainly glad to end her sojourn in primitive Indiana. She later wrote an autobiographical novel in which she described the town of Norton, a thinly veiled fictional Indianapolis. In her book, she wrote that the level land around Norton looked "as if one good, thorough rain would transform it into an impassable morass." She imagined that the residents had to use stilts to get around in rainy weather, and the locale of the city was characterized as a slough. She conceded that the town was "very prettily laid out" with broad, shaded streets, but overall, her account would not win the favor of local boosters.[27] For some residents with loftier ambitions, such as the Beechers, Indianapolis remained a muddy, stump-ridden community of possible potential but not a place for a distinguished clergyman to spend his life.

In 1857 an early history of Indianapolis summarized the first quarter century of the capital's existence. It remarked that "the town had been shut out from the world from the time of its early settlement, by an almost impassable expanse of mud. No business had been transacted other than that of supplying the wants of the few inhabitants." According to this observer, "the effort and risk of reaching [the town] was sufficiently great to appall many travellers." In sum, "a death-like quiet pervaded the place."[28] It was a slumbering community that had not yet awakened.

1847: THE YEAR OF CHANGE

In 1847 the alarm sounded, and Indianapolis finally seemed to wake up. The remaining years of the 1840s witnessed notable changes and an increase of energy and enterprise not previously known in the town. Indianapolis overcame its isolation and surged forward in population. A fresh optimism prevailed as the capital entered a new era and appeared poised to realize its potential.

Indicative of the change was the decision to incorporate as a city. In March 1847, by a vote of 449 to 19, the electorate approved a city charter that replaced the town board of trustees with a mayor and common council of seven members. Indianapolis voters proceeded to elect Samuel Henderson as their first mayor; he had also been the first postmaster and the first president of the town board of trustees. The new city included virtually the entire four-square-mile donation, though much of the land outside the original Mile Square plat remained "pretty good hunting ground for quails and squirrels."[29] The municipal powers of the new city were not much greater than those of the town, but the fact that Indianapolis residents opted for city status testified to the higher aspirations of the community. In Indiana, smaller communities were generally towns; the very term *city* implied a place that was bigger and no longer a country crossroads.

Much more important for the future of the new city was the arrival of the first railroad line in the fall of 1847. Commentators at the time and ever afterward agreed that this was a revolutionary event in the capital's history. Finally, the city would be able to overcome its lack of a navigable waterway. Railroads could transport passengers and freight more cheaply and quickly than wagons on the National Road. Unlike rivers and canals that froze over in the winter, railroads operated year-round. Moreover, they had the potential to reach areas inaccessible to steamboats.

Railroads could relieve the isolation of Indianapolis and turn a community of deathlike quiet into a bustling hub of commerce.

On October 1, 1847, the locomotives and cars of the Madison and Indianapolis Railroad pulled into the capital city. Much to the joy of Indianapolis boosters, the line linked the city to Madison on the Ohio River and ensured access to the great inland river system of North America. According to a local newspaper, "At about 3 o'clock in the afternoon, the belching forth of the loud-mouthed cannon announced the time for the approach of the cars from Madison." A crowd of people thronged the grounds of the depot: "They were there by acres, stretching far out along the railroad, some upon trees, stumps, fences, mounds, and everything which tended to raise one squad above another." People who were picketed down the line spied "a dark spot in the distance" and "heard the shrill whistle of the locomotive, echoing through hoary forests and o'er verdant fields." Once the locomotives turned a curve, spectators could see "two long trains of passenger and freight cars, completely filled with human beings, the ladies waving their white handkerchiefs and the men and boys using their lungs in answering back the long, loud huzzas from the people awaiting their approach."[30]

The governor stood atop one of the cars to give a speech, but the crowd was mainly interested in getting aboard the train for a pleasure ride to nearby Greenwood. Adding to the day's celebration was the arrival of Spalding's North American Circus, which featured "35 widely celebrated lady and gentlemen artistes, at the acme of their profession." Also present was Ned Kendall's brass band of "15 picked musicians in lustrous uniforms," with Kendall himself known for his "never to be forgotten Solo upon his Magic Silver Bugle."[31]

The day closed with fireworks and a performance by Spalding's equestrians. After the disastrous grounding of the *General Robert Hanna* and the failure of the Central Canal project, Indianapolis residents had reason to celebrate. The railroad extended all the way to Madison on the Ohio River; it was not simply a nine-mile ditch running to a nearby village. Moreover, the trains that arrived in Indianapolis could return safely to Madison and continue to operate along the line. This was not a one-time trip, like that of the *General Robert Hanna*. Indianapolis's commercial ambitions were about to be realized.

One month after the arrival of the railroad, an Indianapolis newspaper lauded the new spirit in the city. "Indianapolis is not as it used to be," it reported. "The completion of the rail road has transformed its every feature, and one, looking upon its crowded thoroughfares and listening to the din and confusion of its commerce, could scarce conceive it once had been the 'sweetest village of the plain.'" According to the newspaper, "Indianapolis has changed. Friday, Oct. 1st, 1847, was an era in our history. On that day we were linked with commerce."[32]

Later observers agreed with this assessment. In 1870 the journalist William Holloway attempted to express the momentous significance of the arrival of the railroad: "There came with it ... such a change as comes upon boyhood at puberty. There was a change of features, of form, a suggestion of manhood, a trace of beard and voice of virality."[33] Indianapolis had left behind its puny childhood and was on the verge of becoming a full-grown city.

At the close of the century, a boosterish publication repeated these claims by stating that until the coming of the railroad, "the town was completely isolated, and its life was stagnant." The year 1847, however, "witnessed the wonderful change, and in that year occurred the first of the long chain of events that revolutionized the character of Indianapolis, and ... made it one of the liveliest, progressive and wide awake cities in America."[34]

Embedded in the local psyche was the notion that 1847 was the year of change, the key turning point in the city's history. The frontier village was deemed a thing of the past. Indianapolis had emerged as a city not only in name and form of government. It was finally on the path to becoming a city in reality. One month after the railroad's arrival as well as fifty years later, promoters of the Hoosier capital marked the year of 1847 as a time of transformation.

In 1848 another change occurred that was less celebrated but also instrumental in ending the city's isolation. That year Indianapolis's first telegraph office opened. In May a telegraph line was completed to Dayton, Ohio, and dispatches conveyed by telegraph were published in a local newspaper. Twenty-three years earlier, a Lawrenceburg newspaper had complained that it took nine days to receive reports from Indianapolis. Now there was instantaneous communication with the outside world. As in the case of the railroad, the change seemed revolutionary. Commenting on the telegraph line extending along Washington Street, an early settler who had helped clear the virgin forests in 1821 exclaimed, "Good Lord! who would ever have thought of seeing lightning driven down the street."[35]

The late 1840s also witnessed the development of benevolent institutions in the burgeoning capital. In 1843 Indiana's legislature authorized a property tax to support a state school for the deaf. The school operated in rented quarters while the state constructed an impressive structure to house the State Asylum for the Deaf and Dumb. Opened in 1850, the asylum was east of the Mile Square and consisted of two buildings in the Greek revival style. The principal building was 265 feet long, and its center section rose five stories. It was a stately structure that proudly advertised the benevolence of the Hoosier people. Complete with Doric columns and an octagonal cupola, it was a monumental addition to the emerging capital city.

Meanwhile, the state was building a school for the blind in the northern section of the Mile Square. Like the deaf school, it was in the Greek revival style, with a portico supported by Ionic columns. Whereas the state covered the walls of the state capitol with less expensive and sadly defective stucco, sandstone faced the brick walls of the blind school. In fact, the state spent almost twice as much for the blind school as it did for the capitol.

West of the city, the state constructed the Indiana Hospital for the Insane. Authorized by the legislature in 1847, it received its first patients the following year. Like the other institutions, it testified to the expanding role of the state government. The state was assuming responsibility for its citizens no matter their disability, and most important for Indianapolis, it chose to concentrate its varied benevolent institutions in the capital city.

The census figures of 1850 reflected the new developments transforming Indianapolis. Since 1840 the capital's population had tripled; Indianapolis now had 8,091 residents. Despite this growth, the city still did not stand out as a future great metropolis. In population it ranked eighty-seventh among the nation's cities, slightly smaller than eighty-sixth-ranked Danvers, Massachusetts, and just ahead of Lynchburg, Virginia. Cincinnati, the Midwest's chief metropolis, had 115,000 inhabitants; Saint Louis was home to 75,000 people; and the Ohio capital city of Columbus was still more than twice as populous as the Hoosier seat of government. Though Indianapolis's rate of increase was impressive, it paled next to the more than sixfold rise in Chicago's population. Within Indiana, Indianapolis had moved slightly ahead of Madison, though New Albany remained the largest city in the state. Indianapolis was not yet considered Indiana's chief city. Instead, the Ohio River port of New Albany still held that distinction.

Moreover, not all Indianapolis residents were confident the capital city would ever emerge as a truly significant hub. Samuel Henderson, the city's first postmaster, first president of the town board, and first mayor, decided to give up on the community. In 1850 he sold his property and left Indianapolis to find his fortune in the California gold fields. He had arrived in Indianapolis in the fall of 1821 and had witnessed its emergence from the forests. He had led efforts to further the growth and development of the community, but now he decided to surrender to the city's seemingly inevitable mediocrity. According to a friend, Henderson believed "that the general railroad system being inaugurated would ruin the city; that the thousands of persons who passed through it would not stop long enough to get a drink of water, and that Indianapolis would retrograde, and become nothing but a way station."[36]

Despite the year of change and the optimism of Indianapolis boosters, Henderson was convinced that Indianapolis was destined to be insignificant. This pioneer who had nurtured the community through its founding years was opting for a brighter future far to the west in California.

2

Indianapolis Takes Off
1850–1900

Samuel Henderson was wrong. During the half century follow-ing his departure, Indianapolis took off and advanced from a small country town to a major American city. Indianapolis was finally emerging from the mud, overcoming its past isolation, and achieving a reputation as one of the leading hubs of the booming Midwest. By the close of the century, it was no longer a town despairing of its lack of steamboat or canal traffic. As a rail center, it had become the crossroads of America. Indianapolis was no longer in the middle of nowhere; instead, it was where the paths of commerce met. Investors profited handsomely from the city's growth as land values soared and businesses flourished. It was a real estate mother lode at least equal to Henderson's Cali-fornia gold fields. By the time of Henderson's death in California in 1883, the city's development had most definitely disproved the prophecy of its first mayor. It was a destination, not a way station, and the tens of thousands of people who had moved to Indianapolis were staying for a lifetime.

THE CITY GROWS

The census figures for the second half of the nineteenth century testify to Indianapolis's success. In the 1850s the city more than doubled in population, rising from 8,091 to 18,611. During the Civil War, Indianapolis achieved new importance as a gathering point for Indiana troops headed to the Southern battlefields and as a source of supplies for the Union army. By 1870 the number of residents had nearly tripled to 48,244. According to the 1870 census, a majority of Marion County's population lived in Indianapolis. Marion County was no longer a predominantly rural county; henceforth, its city dwellers far outnumbered its country folk. The national economic depression of the mid-1870s hit Indianapolis especially hard, ruining overly optimistic speculators. Yet the population continued to rise to 75,056 in 1880. In the 1880s and 1890s, Indianapolis benefited from the discovery and exploitation of natural gas fields in the counties to the north-east of the city. By 1890, the capital's population topped 100,000, and it reached 169,164 in 1900. In half a century, the number of inhabitants rose more than twentyfold.

This half century was a period of marked growth for cities throughout the nation. Indianapolis, however, more than kept up with the urban pack, soaring in the ranks of American cities. In 1850 it was the nation's eighty-seventh-largest city; fifty years later it ranked twenty-first. It was the eighth largest city in the Midwest and the third most populous state capital, surpassed by only Boston and Providence. The capital city of Columbus, Ohio, had long paralleled the development of Indianapolis. In 1850, it had more than twice the population of Indianapolis, but in 1900 it had 43,500 fewer residents than the Hoosier capital. The population of Cincinnati had not quite tripled during the half century, while that of Saint Louis had risen less than eightfold. Clearly, Indianapolis was outpacing a number of its midwestern neighbors.

Indianapolis also had finally become the preeminent city in Indiana. After 1850 it no longer trailed New Albany or vied with Madison. By 1900 Indianapolis had nearly three times the population of Evansville, the state's second largest city, and was nearly four times as large as third-ranked Fort Wayne. As the English translation of its name implied, it was Indiana's city, the unquestioned urban hub of the Hoosier state. By 1900 one out of every fifteen Indiana residents lived in the capital city, and its share of the state's rapidly urbanizing population was increasing each decade.

As Indianapolis increased in population, it grew in area. No longer was it confined to the Mile Square of the four-square-mile donation. In mid-1891 its area was 15.03 square miles; on January 1, 1902, after a series of annexations, it was 28.15 square miles. Though still less than one-tenth the area of Marion County, it was consuming expanses of the surrounding countryside at an increasing pace. It was not a small town one could walk across with ease. It was a big city both in population and area.

As Indianapolis grew, it developed distinct neighborhoods and a pattern of economic and social-class segregation. The Mile Square was increasingly devoted to commerce rather than residence. Downtown was where many people worked and shopped but fewer people lived. Residential neighborhoods for the wealthy developed; these were areas where the "best people" lived. This was a commonplace development in cities throughout the nation. Grand avenues of fine homes, manicured lawns, and stately elms became the preserve of those who had succeeded in the fast-growing cities. In Buffalo, the street of distinction was Delaware Avenue; in Cleveland, it was Euclid Avenue; in Detroit, Woodward Avenue was the residential showplace. Indianapolis similarly had its haven for the successful. On the north side, the area bounded by Tenth Street on the south and Sixteenth Street on the north and along Delaware Street, Meridian Street, Broadway, and Park Avenue became the preferred address for the wealthy. During the second half of the nineteenth century, a pattern was developing that was to prevail well into the twenty-first century and probably beyond. The north side was the "best address," and over the decades, the affluent simply migrated farther north. In Indianapolis, money has typically moved north.

Delaware Street's most distinguished residents were Benjamin and Caroline Harrison, and they exemplified the type of people who segregated themselves along the city's preferred avenues. Benjamin Harrison was the grandson of President William Henry Harrison and would himself become the twenty-third

President Harrison's house

president of the United States, serving from 1889 to 1893. A leading attorney in the city, a brevet brigadier general during the Civil War, and an elder of the First Presbyterian Church, he was a model of respectability and a pillar of the established order. Caroline Harrison taught Sunday school, played the organ at the Presbyterian church, and served as a member of the board of managers of the Indianapolis Orphans Asylum. As first lady she was named the first president-general of the Daughters of the American Revolution. She was a woman worthy of her impeccably upright husband. The Harrisons' home on North Delaware Street advertised their economic success and social standing. Constructed in 1876, it was a large brick Italianate manse with a coiffured lawn in keeping with the distinguished character of the neighborhood. The Harrisons personified the ideal of the affluent north side. It was a zone largely reserved for well-to-do models of Victorian respectability.

In contrast, the south side became the working-class area of the city. The less affluent clustered near the growing number of manufacturing establishments south of the Mile Square and created neighborhoods that did not produce presidents of the United States or officers of the Daughters of the American Revolution. South-siders could not afford the homes on North Delaware Street and were cut off from the city center by rail lines. These residents spent their modest incomes in the shops and businesses of a secondary business district that developed around what became known as Fountain Square. This was a working-class hub and testified to the growing class differentiation in the capital city. The north side was for the business leaders; the south side was for their employees and small entrepreneurs not invited into the parlors of North Delaware Street.

Indianapolis's working class, however, did not crowd into notorious multistory tenements, as did their counterparts in New York City. Indianapolis boasted of being "a city of homes," and the data justified this slogan. In 1900 there were only 1.1 families per dwelling in Indianapolis, meaning that few families lived atop one another in the same building. At the close of the century, 94 percent of the dwelling structures in the Hoosier capital were single-family houses. Only 1–2 percent of the residential buildings housed three or more families. Moreover, single-family dwellings in Indianapolis were not rowhouses, as in Philadelphia and Baltimore. On the south side as well as the north side, the typical dwelling was a detached house on an individual lot. No matter their economic or social status, Indianapolis families did not share space with others. They lived in single-family houses with space between themselves and their neighbors.

This did not mean that housing conditions were equal or ideal throughout the city. The working class lived in small frame cottages with no indoor plumbing that bore no resemblance to the north side's turreted, bay-windowed brick manses with elaborate turned spindle work. Less affluent Indianapolis residents did not share an exterior wall with an adjoining structure and were not piled on top of one another in multistory tenements. Their dwellings, however, were at best modest and at worst shacks. Indianapolis boosters proudly proclaimed their hometown as a city of homes, but many of the homes were nothing to brag about.

As Indianapolis sprawled outward from the old Governor's Circle, many residents settled in dwellings beyond the city limits, resulting in the incorporation of a number of suburban municipalities. Perhaps the most distinctive of the new suburbs was Woodruff Place. Platted in 1872 by local businessman-speculator James Woodruff, it was laid out as a residential park with three main drives, each approximately a half mile long. A cross drive connected the three streets. At each of the intersections were fountains. Moreover, running down the center of the drives were landscaped esplanades with statuary, flower beds, shrubs, and trees. It was intended to be a sylvan haven for the families of businessmen and professionals, a refuge from the increasing noise, smoke, and bustle of the growing capital city. The lots were large and well shaded, and residents expected to live at peace with nature. Woodruff Place was designed to be the antithesis of urban.

In 1876 the few Woodruff Place residents chose to incorporate as an independent municipality, though they contracted with the city of Indianapolis for municipal services. It remained a small community, with 161 residents in 1890 and 477 in 1900. Located east of the city, it deviated from the northward movement of wealth. Whereas north-side residents showed off their affluence on prominent thoroughfares such as Delaware and Meridian Streets, the more discreet gentry of Woodruff Place isolated themselves along their landscaped, shaded drives. Yet the community was known as one of the enclaves inhabited by the "best people." Booth Tarkington admitted that Woodruff Place was the setting for his famed novel *The Magnificent Ambersons*. The Ambersons were an old family ill-suited to, and ultimately victimized by, the breakneck growth and industrialization of the midwestern city. Woodruff Place, in reality, was a refuge that turned its back on that growth and devouring development and attempted to nurture an alternative, more peaceful lifestyle.

Farther east was another genteel exception to the northward movement of gentility. This was the community of Irvington. Platted in 1870, it was also intended as a residential suburb, and again the emphasis was on a peaceful existence removed from the hubbub of the urban core. Rather than copying Indianapolis's grid pattern of streets that ran perpendicular to one another, the designers of Irvington opted for a curvilinear scheme. Whereas the straight streets of Indianapolis conformed to the geometric principle that the shortest distance between two points is a straight line, Irvington's curving streets suggested a more leisurely, relaxed mode of life where one was not seeking the shortest distance or the quickest means to get to a destination. In commercial Indianapolis, the goal was to reach a place as quickly as possible and make a profit. Time was money. In suburban Irvington, residents were willing to meander and pursue an existence alien to the big city.

The original deeds to Irvington lots included provisions intended to maintain the desired suburban environment. The purchaser and "his heirs and assigns" agreed not to erect or maintain "any distillery, brewery, soap-factory, pork-house, slaughter-house, or any other establishment offensive to the people." In addition, purchasers would not sell "any intoxicating liquors except for medicinal, sacramental or mechanical purposes strictly."[1] Irvington was to be off-limits to the smell, filth, and sins of the nearby city of Indianapolis.

In 1873, Irvington incorporated as a municipality. Among its first ordinances was one requiring landowners to plant shade trees, another outlawing the shooting of firearms within the municipality, and a provision banning the killing of "any bird within said town."[2] Like Woodruff Place, Irvington residents would enjoy a quiet, safe environment and live in happy accord with nature. Whereas the first Indianapolis residents of fifty years earlier had devoted themselves to clearing the forests and shooting the indigenous wildlife to enhance their diets, their grandchildren in Irvington wished to re-create and preserve nature.

Other suburban municipalities developed to serve expanding industries and provide housing for their workers. The town of Brightwood was platted in 1872 and incorporated in 1876. As the site of the Bee Line Railroad shops and several manufacturing concerns, the town attracted working-class residents. By 1890, its population was 1,387. West Indianapolis developed north of the Indianapolis stockyards, and its history was tied to those yards. Whereas Irvington and Woodruff Place sought to distance themselves from such malodorous establishments, West Indianapolis was dependent on the business generated by the holding of soon-to-be slaughtered cattle and hogs. It did, however, attract working-class residents, reaching a population of 3,527 in 1890. Meanwhile, other workers were settling in Haughville, which grew up around the Haugh, Ketcham and Company Iron Works. Incorporated in 1883, Haughville was not a tranquil suburb of the Woodruff Place ilk. It was a scene of labor discontent and tension between immigrant and African American populations. Not as large as West Indianapolis, it claimed 2,144 residents in 1890.

In 1897 Indianapolis annexed Brightwood, West Indianapolis, and Haughville and proceeded to do the same to Irvington in 1902. None of the communities could equal Indianapolis in municipal services, so the local populations acceded to the territorial ambitions of the big city. Only Woodruff Place survived, not succumbing to annexation until 1962. Indianapolis's neighboring communities were not, then, destined to survive. The city was growing, and small-town governments did not stand in the way of its expansion.

The varied suburban towns also testified to the newly emerging social segregation of the capital region. Indianapolis was no longer a small town where rich and poor lived within walking distance of one another. As the city grew, it developed different zones separated by social chasms. Residents of the south side or Haughville did not frequent Caroline Harrison's parlors except as servants. Moreover, some parts of Indianapolis were beyond the pale of Mrs. Harrison. The expanding city of Indianapolis was a social checkerboard. Its map included the sylvan esplanades of Woodruff Place and the stockyard village of West Indianapolis.

As the city of Indianapolis grew, it had to provide a full range of services that had been unavailable in the earlier frontier village. The former town of Indianapolis had imposed certain restrictions and regulations but had furnished few services. During the second half of the century, as the booming city of Indianapolis became home to more than one hundred thousand residents, it needed to develop professional fire and police forces and provide street lighting, piped water, streetcar service, street pavements, and parks for a growing and demanding urban public. It was no longer a pioneer community with stumps in the streets. Instead, it had emerged as a major city with a municipal government that ensured an up-to-date urban lifestyle.

In 1859 a city ordinance authorized the creation of a paid fire department. Before this time volunteer companies had provided fire protection, but now the city took over and dedicated itself to fashioning a department worthy of a growing city. To warn of fires before they spread, the department maintained a watchtower atop the community's tallest building where a man was stationed with binoculars. If he spied a fire, he would issue the alarm by ringing a bell mounted on the building. In 1868 the department adopted a telegraph alarm system, and by the turn of the century, there were 104 alarm boxes spread throughout the city to carry reports of fires. As the city grew, the number of alarm incidents likewise rose. In 1882 there were 212 alarms, in 1892 the number had increased to 435, and in 1900 the department recorded 1,052 emergency calls. To handle this increase, the department expanded its workforce; in 1895 it included a chief, an assistant chief, and 116 firefighters.

Paralleling the growth of a professional fire department was the emergence of a police force. In 1854 the mayor appointed fourteen men to constitute the city's first police department. Before this time, law and order had been the responsibility of a volunteer night watch aided by the town marshal, the county sheriff, and a few constables. At first the police patrolled only at night, but in 1862 they took on daylight duties. A laudatory account of 1896 assured readers that "the police department of Indianapolis is now fully equal to that of any other city." It was "an able, efficient and well-drilled body of men who have always established their title to be called faithful and heroic conservators of the peace and suppressors of the lawlessness."[3] At that time the department was composed of 124 employees, including eighty-nine patrolmen and a corps of detectives. Like the volunteer firemen, the volunteer night watch was a barely remembered institution of the past. At the close of the century, Indianapolis, like other burgeoning American cities, was served by hundreds of paid municipal employees.

Well-lit streets were deemed a necessity in limiting crime and disorder after sunset. In 1851 the city council granted a fifteen-year exclusive franchise to the Indianapolis Gas Light and Coke Company to provide gas to local customers. The company laid mains along Pennsylvania and Washington Streets and in January 1852 furnished illumination to its first customers. To celebrate the occasion, a local druggist invited Indianapolis residents to see his "gas light sign" with "admittance free, children half price."[4] Between 1853 and 1855, the first gas street lights were erected on the city's main thoroughfares. By 1860, 265 lights lined eight and a half miles of streets.

In 1881 Indianapolis entered the electric light age when the city council contracted with the Indianapolis Brush Electric Light and Power Company. The company was to erect five towers with powerful sixteen-thousand-candlepower arc lights—one in the Governor's Circle and four others at major downtown intersections. Former mayor John Caven, who headed the Brush Company initiative, promised the towers would make Indianapolis "the most splendidly illuminated city in the world, and at the least cost."[5] In 1892 an ordinance specified that the Brush Company was to provide Indianapolis with 750 two-thousand-candlepower arc lights. Gradually electricity was replacing gas light, and the municipal council was expelling darkness from the capital city.

Meanwhile, the council was also furnishing water to the expanding population. Most major American cities built municipal-owned waterworks, but Indianapolis deviated from the norm by contracting with a private water company. In 1870 the Water Works Company of Indianapolis secured a franchise to build and operate a waterworks and lay pipes to distribute the water. Many residents preferred to rely on their own wells, and the company suffered hard times. In 1881 the Indianapolis Water Company took over the waterworks, and gradually consumers opted for a more modern water supply. Indianapolis, however, was not in the forefront of water technology and lagged behind many large American cities. In 1896 the boosterish publication that lauded the local police force had to admit that the city's water supply was not all that could "be desired in so far as quantity [was] concerned." But, it claimed, "this defect is being rapidly remedied."[6]

Indianapolis was, however, keeping up with rival cities in the field of streetcar transportation. In January 1864 the city council granted a thirty-year franchise to construct and operate streetcar lines to the Citizens Street Rail Road Company. By October of that year, the first line was in operation. According to a local newspaper, "This marks an era in the history of our city as significant as it is gratifying." Horses or mules pulled the cars along the rails, so passengers traveled at a slow gait. Indianapolis had not entered an age of rapid transit. Yet another newspaper proclaimed, "[The] operations of a mule horse railway . . . are magnificent, and the public, at five cents a piece, appreciate their performance." Aware of the animal droppings that resulted from streetcar transport, the newspaper noted that "shovels and carts [would] hereafter follow in the wake."[7]

The system expanded rapidly, and by the close of 1868, the Citizens line averaged 550 round trips daily, transporting four thousand passengers. There were already more than fifteen miles of rails and fifty cars, and sixty-four men and 150 mules and horses were employed. Animal power, however, was not sufficient for the rapidly growing cities of the late nineteenth century. In 1890 the Citizens Company began electrifying its lines. Henceforth,

Electric streetcars downtown, 1896

electric power to propel trolleys would supplant the horses and mules. Celebrating the change, newspaper headlines trumpeted, "The Mules Have Gone."[8] Expressing their support for the new technology, a crowd of Indianapolis transit riders cheered the arrival of the first electric streetcar on the city streets. Electrification proceeded at a rapid pace. By the close of 1893, the city could claim 80.81 miles of electric track and only 14.38 miles of animal lines. In 1894 electricity displaced most of the remaining mules. The electric lines were not only cleaner than their animal-powered counterparts, they also furnished faster transportation. Consequently, residents could commute farther from the city center, opting for homes along the urban fringe. Advances in transportation thus promoted the expansion of the city. In 1850 most Indianapolis residents moved about the town on foot. They could only commute as far as they could comfortably walk. By 1900 they could board an electric streetcar and escape to homes miles from the urban core.

One of the most troublesome municipal endeavors of the second half of the nineteenth century was street paving. Cities, including Indianapolis, experimented with various surfaces, opting for wooden blocks, cobblestones, and macadam pavements. The results varied but were rarely optimal. By 1890 Indianapolis's leading citizens realized that something more needed to be done. That year a group of businessmen dissatisfied with the state of the city, led by Colonel Eli Lilly, formed the Commercial Club. Intended to improve and promote the rapidly expanding capital city, the club focused first on the paving issue. If Indianapolis was truly to take its place among the nation's great cities, it had to improve its street surfaces. Wooden blocks that sank in the mud were not adequate, and neither were old-fashioned cobblestone streets or unpaved thoroughfares.

Responding to the perceived crisis, the Commercial Club sponsored a National Street Paving Exposition in Indianapolis in April 1890. The club invited leading paving contractors and manufacturers of street-paving materials to come to the city and explain and promote their products and services. They would thereby educate Indianapolis citizens about what could be done to improve the city's streets. Twelve thousand people attended the exposition, and representatives from forty cities heard fifty-five exhibitors discuss various paving materials.

The exposition produced positive results. By the 1890s asphalt and brick were emerging as the best options for street surfacing, and the newly energized city of Indianapolis readily embraced these materials. In 1891 the mileage of asphalt streets more than tripled; at the close of the year, there were five and three-quarter miles of asphalt pavement. In addition, the city constructed nearly two miles of brick streets. The following year Indianapolis laid nearly three additional miles of asphalt pavement and nearly five miles of brick surfaces. Indianapolis was applying the best materials available, and by 1900 the principal streets of the Hoosier capital matched those of other major cities in the United States.

Though Indianapolis was making progress with street paving during the early 1890s, it was still lagging behind other cities in park development. Until the mid-1890s the city council was relatively indifferent to the desirability of furnishing public spaces for relaxation and recreation. The state-owned Military Park and University Square offered some greenery and sylvan relief from the bustle of the growing capital. But at the time the city owned only one park. That was Garfield Park, opened in 1876 on the south side and largely neglected by the city council during the following two decades. A later commentator reported that Garfield Park in the 1890s "was rather a joke as a park."[9]

In 1895, however, Thomas Taggart assumed the office of mayor and committed himself to the creation of a public park system. In 1897 the city council authorized the acquisition of 953 acres to form Riverside Park and 82 acres for Brookside Park. As its name implied, Riverside Park was along the banks of the White River and testified to an emerging desire to preserve and embellish the city's natural features for the uplift of the urban public. By the turn of the century, Indianapolis was finally realizing that a rapidly growing city needed to set aside natural preserves rather than become an unrelieved expanse of buildings and pavements.

During the last decades of the century, the state of Indiana was also acting to make its capital city a source of pride. Most notably, it built a grand new capitol building to replace the structure that had been completed in 1835. The old statehouse was literally crumbling by the 1860s. In 1867 the ceiling of the chamber of the house of representatives collapsed. Jacob Dunn, a journalist and local historian, remembered that as a youth, he "climbed over the debris and rescued the hands of the [house of representatives] clock, which had been smashed in the catastrophe." The chamber was "a magnificent wreck." According to Dunn, before the old statehouse "was replaced it acquired the appearance of a genuine Grecian ruin."[10] Clearly, the state and its capital city needed something better.

In 1877 the state legislature bowed to necessity and authorized the governor to appoint a four-person commission to build a new capitol costing no more than $2 million. In August of that year, the commission sold the old statehouse for $250 with the understanding that the purchaser would remove the derelict building by April 1878. Meanwhile, the commissioners examined twenty-four plans submitted by architects and chose the submission of Edwin May of Indianapolis. In 1879 the legislature was relegated to the Marion County Courthouse as excavation began on the new capitol's basement. Amid ceremony, the cornerstone was laid in 1880, and construction proceeded until completion in 1888.

The new structure was an edifice worthy of the state and its burgeoning capital city. Nearly five hundred feet in length, it was topped by a dome rising 234 feet. As the most important building in Indianapolis, it appropriately dominated the skyline of the low-rise city. Its exterior walls were brick covered in Indiana limestone, and Corinthian columns and pilasters added to the grandeur of the building. The ornate interior was in the Italian Renaissance style, and an art-glass inner dome of predominantly blue tones soared above the central rotunda, making it the most striking part of the statehouse. Unlike the older capitol, it was not a product of shoddy workmanship. According to a contemporary account, "The commissioners have watched the progress of the work incessantly, and anxiously, and have secured . . . as perfect a piece of builders' skill as can be found in any modern structure in Christendom."[11]

In 1887 the state embarked on another project that would further Indianapolis's image as a grand capital city. That year the legislature authorized a commission to plan and guide the

The Soldiers and Sailors Monument

construction of a memorial to Indiana's heroic war dead. The commission advertised an international competition for the design of the Soldiers and Sailors Monument and in 1888 chose the submission of Bruno Schmitz of Berlin, Germany, as the winning entry. The new monument was to be located at the heart of the capital in the Governor's Circle, which henceforth would be known as Monument Circle. Over the next fourteen years, construction proceeded on the limestone monument, which rose 248 feet, exceeding the new capitol in height. A statue of Victory added 30 feet to the top of the tower. Three bronze astragals encircled the monument, and at the base were four giant groups of statuary that represented war, peace, the dying soldier, and the return home. The German sculptor Rudolf Schwarz fashioned these pieces as well as statues representing the infantry, cavalry, artillery, and navy. Four bronze statues of figures important in the wars during Indiana's history added to the array of sculpture. Huge candelabras and cascading fountains completed the awesome ensemble.

At the very center of the city, the Soldiers and Sailors Monument was the most impressive war memorial in the nation. It proclaimed Indiana's patriotic pride in a grand manner and became the capital city's iconic landmark. With the abundance of statuary and the soaring tower topped by Victory, it made clear to any visitor to the city that Indianapolis was reaching for greatness. It was not a humble heartland town hiding its success. It was a city with a patriotic monument worthy of a European capital that surpassed anything rival cities could boast.

The Soldiers and Sailors Monument was the capstone of a half century of phenomenal transformation. The Indianapolis of 1900 would be unrecognizable to anyone transported from 1850. Its population had grown twentyfold, it had annexed territory well beyond the original four-square-mile donation, electric streetcars plied its asphalt streets, and professional firefighters and police officers protected the lives and property of its citizens. From 1889 to 1893, an Indianapolis man occupied the White House; Indianapolis had risen to the top of the political heap.

Moreover, the new statehouse was an object of pride, unlike the embarrassing edifice of 1835. For decades to come, the Soldiers and Sailors Monument served as a symbol of Indianapolis, and it certainly proclaimed the emergence of the Indiana capital as an American city that could not be ignored.

ECONOMIC DEVELOPMENT

Underlying the transformation of Indianapolis were notable changes in the city's economy. During the second half of the nineteenth century, Indianapolis became a hub of transportation, manufacturing, wholesaling, and retailing. In the early 1840s, it was simply a state capital with just enough workshops and stores to serve the local population. It shipped and sold little to the outside world. Fifty years later it was a major commercial center that also happened to be state capital. Its chief business was no longer legislation but industrial production and the distribution of goods. It was not only one of the largest midwestern cities in terms of population, it was one of the premier business hubs of the heartland.

Railroads were essential to the transformation of the city and its accelerated economic development. The late 1840s and early 1850s witnessed a rapid increase in the number of rail lines linking Indianapolis to the outside world. By 1855 seven lines converged on the city. Central Indiana was suited to rail construction and transportation. With its level terrain and lack of obstructive mountain ranges or broad navigable rivers necessitating expensive bridge projects, it offered few impediments to the building of railroads. Moreover, its rich farmland produced an ample supply of freight for the expanding number of railcars. It could supply the business necessary for a rail company to reap a profit.

By the late 1850s, Indianapolis promoters were well aware of the great advantage the railroads offered and celebrated the city as a transportation center of great potential. In 1856 local leader Oliver Smith announced, "Such has already been the concentration of railroads at our Capital, that Indianapolis has by common consent received the name of 'the Railroad City of the West.'"[12]

Union Station

Two years later he wrote, "Indianapolis and our railroads present upon the map, an appearance not unlike the hub and spokes of the wheel of a wagon—the roads, like the spokes, running from the center to the circumference in every direction."[13] The *Indiana State Gazetteer* of 1858–1859 was equally enthusiastic about the transportation advantages of the "Railroad City." According to this publication, "The citizens . . . of eighty of the ninety-one counties in the State can leave their homes, visit Indianapolis, attend to business, and return the same day." It estimated "that from three to four thousand persons visit[ed] the city every twenty-four hours, and that nearly one hundred different trains pass[ed] in and out of the city daily."[14]

Facilitating the travel of these passengers was Indianapolis's Union Station, the first of its kind in the nation. In other cities each rail line maintained its own depot; if passengers needed to transfer from one line to another, they had to leave the depot where they had arrived and cross town to the other line's terminal. In 1850 the city council authorized the building of a union track connecting the various lines entering the city. This track carried the passengers from all lines to a single union depot, which opened on the south side of the Mile Square in 1853. Reporting on its opening, a local newspaper commented, "The inauguration was attended by a goodly array of travelers from the various Railroads and many of our citizens drawn there by the novelty of the scene. It was a lively sight—one that did the eyes good."[15]

As the nation's first union depot, the Indianapolis station also drew admiring comments from visitors to the city. In 1857 a traveler from Virginia wrote in his diary, "The bustle & crowd of the Indianapolis Depot exceeds anything I ever heard of. About 6 or 7 long trains were just on the eve of leaving—whilst I suppose full 10,000 people were hurrying & running about." He concluded, "The New York Depots are not to be compared with it."[16] A decade earlier a deathlike quiet had pervaded the place; by 1857, however, Indianapolis was a city of noteworthy bustle. Its Union Station surpassed the depots of the nation's largest city.

In coming decades, the traffic increased and the number of passengers multiplied. After the Civil War, additional rail companies opted to serve the city, and eventually sixteen lines entered Indianapolis. In 1866 it was necessary to build an addition to Union Station, and in 1888 an even larger and grander depot replaced the original structure. The new station was the pride of the city. A notable example of the then-fashionable Romanesque revival architecture, its lofty tower advertised to travelers the importance of the building and the city it served. The depot's three-story vaulted waiting room was the building's most impressive space and a tribute to the railroad's transformative role in the history of the city. By the close of the century, this hub of rail travel served two hundred passenger trains daily.

By the 1870s the increase in rail traffic resulted in congestion along the union tracks; railcars blocked the city streets, impeding the movement of pedestrians and vehicles. Consequently, support developed for the construction of a beltline along the outskirts of the city that would connect all the railroads and divert freight traffic from the city center. The completed Belt Railroad ran around the east, west, and south sides of the city and enabled freight to pass readily from one line to another. Moreover, it encouraged the development of new outlying factory sites. A location along the Belt Railroad facilitated the nationwide shipment of any company's manufactures.

The promoters of the Belt Railroad also developed a stockyard along the new line. This vast yard for the marketing of livestock took advantage of Indianapolis's admirable rail system and proved another example of the city's business success. From 1877 to January 1902, the yards received more than 27 million swine, 2.9 million cattle and an equal number of sheep, and 400,000 horses. Located at the center of rich midwestern farm country and having rail facilities surpassed by few cities, Indianapolis developed into a major hub for the selling and distribution of a multitude of livestock.

Indianapolis was emerging not only as a transportation center but also as a major manufacturing city. As the promoters of the steam mill discovered in the 1830s, large-scale manufacturing could not prosper if there was no means of shipping products to out-of-town markets. The isolated, landlocked town of the 1830s had not been linked to the necessary distribution network. However, the railroad city of the late nineteenth century had the means of distributing to customers throughout the nation. With railroads running like spokes in all directions, Indianapolis met a vital requirement for manufacturing success. Further enhancing its qualification for industrial development was its central location. In the early 1830s, Indianapolis was on the edge of settlement, removed from the nation's population centers. Yet by 1890 the nation's center of population was in Decatur County, Indiana, and in 1900 it had moved about fifteen miles to the west to Bartholomew County, Indiana. At the close of the century, Indiana was, then, at the heart of the American market. Indianapolis was no longer off the beaten track; it was in the heart of it all. No major city was more centrally located to the nation's population with railroads that could readily access millions of American consumers. To add to the city's advantages was its access to fuel. Fifty miles to the southwest were seemingly inexhaustible coalfields. Coal was the chief fuel of the age, and southwestern Indiana could boast enough of it to power a multitude of industries in the capital city.

Indianapolis, then, was connected at the very heart of the American market and was well supplied with the source of energy necessary to late nineteenth-century manufacturers. Whereas in the early 1830s it had none of the qualifications for manufacturing success, sixty years later it was in an ideal position to become an industrial dynamo. By 1900 Indianapolis was not simply the Railroad City, it was also a manufacturing metropolis, the maker of a wide variety of goods sold throughout the United States and the world.

Census data testified to the growth of manufacturing in Indianapolis. In 1880 there were 688 manufacturing establishments in the city; in 1900 that number had increased to 1,910. In 1880 the city's manufacturers employed approximately 10,000 wage earners; in 1900 there were 25,500 manufacturing workers. During the final two decades of the century, manufacturing was the chief source of employment in Indianapolis, with approximately 35–36 percent of the workforce engaged in the industrial sector. Indianapolis had become a predominantly manufacturing city.

Perhaps the most notable manufacturing concern was Kingan and Company, a major pork and beef packer. Established in Indianapolis in 1863, Kingan was killing about five hundred thousand hogs yearly by the early 1880s. It dispatched the animals with speed and efficiency. According to a contemporary account, "An unbroken stream of dead hogs, alive and squealing ten seconds before, pours along the tables from the sticking-pens to the scalding-troughs and scraping-machines incessantly from daylight to dark, and often longer." The dead hogs moved on to a department "in which a crowd of men swing[ed] up and down incessantly flashing cleavers, in a wild, stormy fashion, with no measure or rest." This observer reported that "in 1878 and in 1880 Indianapolis was the third pork-packing point in the world, being exceeded only by Chicago and Cincinnati."[17] Kingan did not slacken its pace over the following two decades. At the turn of the century, it was slaughtering over one million hogs annually and employed about 1,500 to 2,000 workers in its bloody business. About one-third of Kingan's production was exported to Europe and especially to Great Britain. In the 1820s and 1830s, Indianapolis could not ship profitably to anywhere outside of Marion County. Seventy years later it was supplying hams to customers on the other side of the world.

Other Indianapolis concerns were also achieving industrial success. In 1876 Nordyke and Marmon Company moved to Indianapolis from its original location in Richmond, Indiana, seeking to exploit the superior shipping facilities of the Railroad City. At the close of the century, it was recognized as the world's largest maker of flour and cereal milling machinery. In 1856 Elias C. Atkins began his business in a small wooden building measuring

Eli Lilly and Company production plant

sixteen feet by twenty feet. By 1900 E. C. Atkins and Company was one the largest makers of saws in the country and employed about nine hundred workers. The brothers David and Thomas Parry began making two-wheeled road carts in Rushville, Indiana, but moved their business to Indianapolis in 1886. In 1890 they began the large-scale manufacture of four-wheel carriages, surreys, and wagons. Like the Atkins company, the Parry concern became one of the nation's largest manufacturers in its field. Three local breweries merged in 1889 to form the Indianapolis Brewing Company. At the turn of the century, it was producing five hundred thousand barrels of beer annually with a workforce of about one thousand. Founded in Indianapolis in 1882, the Van Camp Packing Company began producing its famed pork and beans in the 1890s, and by 1898 it was marketing six million cans annually.

Colonel Eli Lilly was another leading Indianapolis manufacturer. In 1876 he founded Eli Lilly and Company, a small pharmaceutical business that prospered over the following two decades. By the 1890s it was not as large as Nordyke and Marmon or the

Kingan and Company, but Lilly had emerged as a respected business figure in the city, as demonstrated by his leadership of the Commercial Club. Buoying the Lilly company's profits were sales of Succus Alterans, a supposed remedy for venereal disease derived from a secret recipe of roots and herbs handed down by the Creek Indians. Later investigation found it was not as effective as the Lilly company had originally thought. But it had launched the pharmaceutical firm on the path to future greatness.

During the second half of the nineteenth century, Indianapolis thus developed a broad range of industries. Its manufacturing sector was highly diverse, with successful producers of everything from milling machinery and saws to beer, pork and beans, and pharmaceuticals. Whereas Pittsburgh was winning a reputation as the steel city, Minneapolis was known as the flour milling capital, and Detroit in future decades would become the motor city, Indianapolis was not associated with any one industry. It had a diverse manufacturing base, and this diversity persisted in coming decades. Indianapolis was seemingly a maker of almost everything. Its future prosperity did not depend on any one product.

Manufacturing, however, was not the only growing sector of the city's economy. With its superb network of rail links, Indianapolis was an optimal location for wholesaling. Consequently, the number of wholesale houses burgeoned after the Civil War, many of them clustering in a wholesale district on the near south side in the vicinity of Union Station. By 1900, an estimated 350 Indianapolis wholesale jobbers served the many retailers in small-town Indiana, providing them with the merchandise essential to their businesses.

For example, Hibben, Holloway and Company was a successful importer and wholesaler of "dry goods, notions, [and] woolens"; at the turn of the century, it was purportedly "the oldest and largest jobbing dry goods and notion house in the state."[18] It occupied a group of adjoining buildings in the heart of the city's wholesale district, including one with five floors and another of six stories used for storage. Anyone passing the complex of buildings comprising Hibben, Holloway and Company would be well aware of the city's emergence as a wholesaling hub.

A few blocks north of the wholesale district was Washington Street, the unsurpassed retailing center of the city. The widest thoroughfare of Alexander Ralston's Mile Square, Washington Street became the city's chief place to spend money, as was evident from the throngs of female shoppers crowding the sidewalks as they moved from one store to the next. The emporiums lining the street were not the simple general stores of the past, carrying whatever merchandise could be transported by wagon from Cincinnati. Instead, they were enterprising retail establishments competing for consumer dollars by claiming to offer the finest array of goods imported from throughout the world. And they advertised bargain prices. Thus, the growing number of largely female Indianapolis shoppers were in an admirable position to obtain the best the world offered at a reasonable cost.

One of the chief retailers of the late nineteenth century was the New York Store on Washington Street. Its dramatic four-story central atrium was a showplace of the city and was intended as awe-inspiring proof that there was no other retailer in Indianapolis that could match the New York Store. The emporium also claimed to have "the longest dress goods aisle in the United States" on its first floor and provided elevators to transport shoppers to the rich trove of merchandise on the upper stories.[19]

Among the other Washington Street outlets were retailers that would later develop into the city's largest department stores. In 1872 L. S. Ayres bought a controlling interest in the existing Trade Palace dry goods store, thus founding L. S. Ayres and Company. Like the atrium of the New York Store, the grand central stairway of the Ayres store made clear to customers that this was not an ordinary establishment. It was someplace special that offered the finest shopping experience. An advertisement in 1896 boasted, "This firm was the first in Indianapolis to make a specialty of strictly high-class dry goods."[20] After a remodeling of the store in the late 1890s, one enthusiastic Indianapolis matron shopping at Ayres exclaimed, "Can you imagine you are in Indianapolis amid all this! I feel as if I were in New York or Chicago in one of the big stores."[21]

Another nascent department store was H. P. Wasson and Company. In 1874 Hiram P. Wasson became a partner in the Bee Hive Dry Goods store and nine years later became the sole owner of the establishment that was to bear his name. Like Ayres, the Wasson emporium was a landmark on Washington Street and a mecca for the city's shoppers. In 1896 William H. Block opened a small store on East Washington that, in coming decades, would grow into a major rival of Ayres's and Wasson's establishments.

A wide range of specialty stores completed the shopping experience on Washington Street. Charles Mayer and Company specialized in fine china, glass, and sterling silver as well as toys, toiletries, perfumes, and what Victorians deemed "fancy goods." It proudly offered the finest imports from throughout Europe. George J. Marott's shoe store claimed to have an unequaled inventory of footwear, attracting customers from both Indianapolis and out of town. L. Strauss and Company won a loyal clientele seeking the best in men's clothing, and Washington Street's Vonnegut Company furnished the community with every imaginable type of hardware.

As the shopper at Ayres recognized, Indianapolis retailers were rivaling the best stores in the larger cities of New York and Chicago. Indiana's capital was no longer a backwater town remote from the arteries of commerce. It was a major American hub with retail options worthy of a big city. The very name of the New York Store proclaimed to shoppers that it was an emporium that could take its place among the retailers of the nation's largest city. Indianapolis retailers were asserting their parity with the best the nation could offer.

Unfortunately, not all Indianapolis residents could afford to indulge in the fancy goods at Charles Mayer and Company or the high-class dry goods at Ayres. The working-class residents of the south side, Haughville, and West Indianapolis earned modest wages when employed and struggled to pay their bills.

In 1891–1892 the state's department of statistics recorded the comments of hard-pressed workers. An Indianapolis iron worker complained, "A man can not dress as a citizen of the United States ought to, nor can he have enough to eat and save anything if he pays all his honest debts." A laborer from the city agreed: "A man don't get wages enough to enable him to pay for provisions and clothing."[22] The gap between the well-to-do and the less affluent seemed to be growing and fueling anger among those at the bottom of the social heap. Washington Street was a symbol of the city's material success, and many of its merchants were profiting handsomely. Both Ayres and Wasson owned homes near the Harrisons on North Delaware Street. But there were many other Indianapolis residents who believed they were not getting their fair share of the dividends produced by the city's growth.

Indianapolis was not a center of labor radicalism equal to Chicago. Anarchists found few if any recruits in the Indiana capital, and there was no major socialist movement. Yet there were signs of labor unrest. In 1877 a railroad strike swept through the nation as railway employees walked off the job in protest of wage cuts. Indianapolis workers joined in the strike, paralyzing rail transportation throughout the state. A federal district court judge intervened in what he deemed a critical, dangerous situation and organized a committee of public safety, one of whose members was future president Benjamin Harrison. Harrison assumed charge of a citizen's militia corps intended to maintain order, and the federal judge called on President Rutherford B. Hayes to send federal troops to the Indiana capital. The judge ordered the strikers to return to work, and most complied. Thus, the strike in Indianapolis collapsed without bloodshed or serious disorder.

In 1893 another strike halted streetcar traffic in the city. When the streetcar company attempted to run their cars in defiance of the strikers, they were met with angry crowds of thousands of people. The police attempted to control the mob, arresting more than eighty persons. Protesters hurled mud and rocks at the cars, and among the mob were small girls and boys who reportedly "cursed like little wretches."[23] Eventually management and labor settled their differences, and streetcar transportation returned to normal.

To defend their interests, Indianapolis workers organized unions, and by the 1880s, there were nearly ten thousand union members in the city. In 1892 the Indianapolis General Labor Union claimed eleven thousand members in eighty-three locals. Though not as violent or radical as workers in some cities, the Indianapolis working class did not passively accept their economic fate. They organized and expected a just share of the city's economic benefits.

Because of its central location and optimal accessibility by rail, Indianapolis attracted a number of national union headquarters. In the mid-1870s the Journeyman Stonecutters' Association of North America established its head office in the city. From 1876 to 1880, Indianapolis was the headquarters of the Brotherhoods of Locomotive Firemen, and in 1880 the city attracted the International Typographical Union from New York City. Then, in 1898, the United Mine Workers of America chose Indianapolis for its head office. For a short time in the 1890s, the overarching American Federation of Labor, headed by famed leader Samuel Gompers, maintained its headquarters in Indianapolis before moving to Washington, DC.

During the last decades of the nineteenth century, Indianapolis emerged as a center of labor organizing as well as retailing, wholesaling, manufacturing, and rail traffic. The half century from 1850 to 1900 was a period of extraordinary economic growth and development. The city was finally achieving the economic promise that had eluded its early settlers. In 1900 it was a big city in population, but it also had finally become a formidable city in trade and industry.

THE DIVERSE CITY

Contributing to the rapid growth of Indianapolis was the influx of new residents from Europe. Millions of Europeans migrated to the United States in the second half of the nineteenth century, and a disproportionate share settled in the nation's cities. Indianapolis did not attract as large or diverse an immigrant population as many other cities north of the Mason-Dixon Line. In 1870, 22.1 percent of the Indianapolis population was foreign born, as compared to 44.5 percent in New York City, 48.4 percent in Chicago, and 36.8 percent in Cincinnati. By 1900 the foreign-born share of the Indianapolis population had fallen to 10.1 percent, whereas the figures for New York City, Chicago, and Cincinnati were 37.5 percent, 34.6 percent, and 17.8 percent respectively. By the beginning of the twentieth century, Indianapolis promoters were boasting that the Hoosier capital was a thoroughly American city with less of the corrupting heterogeneity polluting many urban hubs.

Yet the influx of European immigrants to Indianapolis could not be ignored. Thousands of newcomers from abroad were settling in Indianapolis and having a major impact on the growing city. Though far outnumbered by the native born, the European immigrants were vital to the city's rapid ascent to big-city status. By the closing decades of the nineteenth century, Indianapolis was no longer a homogeneous Hoosier town. It was a polyglot city with a rich mixture of people.

Especially significant were the German immigrants. Throughout the second half of the nineteenth century, they were by far the largest immigrant group in Indianapolis and they left an indelible mark on the city's life and culture. From 1870 to 1900, Germans constituted about one-half of the city's foreign-born population, and by 1890 about 28 percent of the city's residents were either German born or children of a German-born parent. With its substantial German element, Indianapolis was typical of the Midwest. The nation's heartland was German country. In cities ranging from Cleveland in the East to Omaha in the West, Germans were the largest foreign-born population in the late nineteenth century. As in Cincinnati, Saint Louis, and Milwaukee, the Teutonic influence was strong in late nineteenth-century Indianapolis.

Das Deutsche Haus

During the 1850s the rapid growth of the German population already had an impact on the capital city. In 1855 the nativist American Party, also known as the Know-Nothing Party, won the city elections. Dedicated to restricting immigration and denying the franchise to many of the foreign born, the party's adherents did not welcome the flood of Germans engulfing Indianapolis. The Know-Nothing victory thus reflected native-born antagonism to alien influences. Especially controversial was the question of the prohibition of alcohol. The Germans were fond of beer and wine and deemed their consumption necessary to a good life, whereas many of Indianapolis's native-born residents regarded alcohol as an evil that should be banned. The Know-Nothing Party's success, however, was short lived, and a state law prohibiting the sale and manufacture of intoxicating beverages was soon held unconstitutional. Yet conflict over the liquor issue persisted throughout the remainder of the century, with the German population steadfastly on the side of personal freedom, including the freedom to drink.

The freedom-loving German community also embraced the antislavery cause. Whereas many of Indianapolis's native-born residents had roots in the Southern slave states and were wary of abolitionists, the German newcomers lined up behind the antislavery forces in the new Republican Party. Indianapolis Germans supported Abraham Lincoln in the 1860 presidential election and rallied behind the Union during the Civil War, organizing a German regiment to fight for the preservation of their new homeland.

Their dedication to the Union did not, however, preclude their devotion to the culture of their European fatherland. The German immigrants were loyal Americans, but they intended to transplant the best of Germany to the United States—and, more specifically, to the Hoosier capital. As early as 1851, the newcomers to Indianapolis formed a turnverein. Proclaiming the importance of a healthy body as well as a healthy mind, the Turner movement swept through Germany in the early nineteenth century and spawned a devotion to physical exercise. The Indianapolis turnverein, like the Turners in the fatherland, promoted gymnastics, but it also served as a welcome refuge for Germans in the somewhat alien Hoosier city. In the post–Civil War decades, the Indianapolis Turner movement flourished. In 1893 the turnverein broke ground for a new clubhouse to be known as Das Deutsche Haus. Completed in 1898, it was a monument of the success and dedication of the local German community. Besides club rooms, Das Deutsche Haus included a gymnasium, a large auditorium, a restaurant, and a biergarten.

A German-language press further perpetuated the culture of the fatherland. As early as 1848, a German immigrant founded the weekly *Indiana Volksblatt*, and in 1853 the *Freie Presse* began publication. There followed additional German-language newspapers, most notably the daily *Taeglicher Telegraph* and the *Indiana Tribuene*. In all, Indianapolis was to become home to twenty-six German-language periodicals, including religious weeklies and monthlies. The German residents of Indianapolis clearly had no desire to abandon their native tongue. The result was an increasingly bilingual city.

Indianapolis Germans were also dedicated to preserving their musical heritage. As early as 1850, an Indianapolis newspaper observed, "The Germans far excel the Americans in musical attainments for the reason they pursue a knowledge of the 'divine art' with industry."[24] The history of music in Indianapolis during the following half century lent strong support to this generalization. Germans enhanced life in the city through their dedication to singing societies and their general love of music. The newcomers were dedicated to raising the level of culture in the city and not acceding to the ways of tone-deaf Americans.

The first of the German singing societies was the Maennerchor, founded in 1854. During the following decades, the all-male Maennerchor presented concerts from October to May as well as summer festivals at outdoor locations. In 1867 it hosted a songfest of the Nord-Amerikanischer Saengerbund (North American Singers' Union). Forty-one musical societies with 798 delegates met in Indianapolis, coming from cities throughout Indiana and Ohio, with representatives from Chicago, West Virginia, and Pennsylvania attending as well. Commenting on the festive event, one attendee wrote, "Indianapolis has put on a festive gown. The business houses downtown are lavishly decorated, the star-spangled banner is flying everywhere and next to it the black-red-gold tricolor of the old Fatherland. . . . 'Welcome Singers' greet us from all windows in English or in German."[25] The singing society proved so successful that in 1878, it moved to the old city hall and transformed it into Maennerchor Hall, which served as the group's permanent performance venue. Meanwhile, Indianapolis Germans founded additional singing societies. In 1870 disgruntled members of the Maennerchor organized the Lyra Society with an orchestra and chorus, and two years later the Liederkranz chorus appeared.

Germans were not only leading figures in the musical life of the city, they were also significant in the economic development of Indianapolis. They were disproportionately represented in the skilled trades and formed a much smaller share of the lowest unskilled occupations. In 1880, 60 percent of the city's brewers and maltsters were German born, as were nearly half the butchers and one-third of the bakers, boot- and shoemakers, and cabinetmakers and upholsterers. In contrast, only 11 percent of the city's laborers and 6 percent of the domestic servants were German born. German American establishments lined the capital city's thoroughfares; in 1875 there were ninety-one German businesses along three prime blocks of Washington Street. There was also a strong German presence in the secondary business district that developed around Fountain Square. Poppe's grocery, the Buddenbaum grocery, Yorger's meat market, and Lorber's saloon all served the German population inhabiting the Fountain Square neighborhood.

Some German Americans proved more successful than the butchers, bakers, and small-scale shopkeepers. The Frenzel family assumed control of the Merchants National Bank and entered the ranks of Indianapolis's business elite. Clemens Vonnegut profited handsomely from his hardware business, and Christian Schmidt and Peter Lieber established major breweries. By 1900 the Frenzel, Vonnegut, and Lieber families were among the most prominent in the city. Economic success in Indianapolis was not an Anglo-American monopoly.

Among the German newcomers to Indianapolis were a relatively small number of Jews. The first Jews settled in Indianapolis in 1849, and by 1860 the Jewish population had increased to about 180. In 1856 fourteen Jewish men met and founded the Indianapolis Hebrew Congregation. As the Jewish population rose markedly during the 1860s, the number of congregants likewise increased, and in 1865 construction began on the Market Street Temple. Attending the elaborate cornerstone ceremony were Indiana's governor, the mayor of Indianapolis, and members of the city council. Indianapolis Jews were clearly not pariahs or outsiders shunned by the Gentile community. The highest public officials were willing to join them in celebrating their new temple.

In fact, the Jewish newcomers quickly established themselves in the city's business community. The Indianapolis city directory of 1859 listed eighteen clothing stores in the city; of these, ten were Jewish owned. During the 1860s, Jews owned an estimated 70 percent of Indianapolis's clothing establishments. Throughout the remainder of the century, the same pattern prevailed. In 1882 half of the city's employed Jews were retailers, shopkeepers, or wholesalers, and most of the other half were employed in such related fields as tailoring and peddling.

Some Jews achieved marked economic success and ranked among the city's business leaders. The clothing merchant Leopold Strauss of L. Strauss and Company was a founder of the Indianapolis Merchants' Association and one of the most prominent retailers along Washington Street. In 1894 the *Indianapolis News* listed the Jewish merchants Leopold Strauss and Herman Bamberger among Indianapolis's leaders. Among the Jewish immigrants was William H. Block, whose small establishment of the 1890s would develop into one of the city's leading department stores. Jewish resident Samuel Rauh founded a series of successful enterprises and in 1897 became president of the Belt Railroad and Stock Yards Company, a mainstay of the city's economy. Henry Kahn established a tailoring business; by 1898 it was so successful that it filled a four-story building in a prime location on Washington Street. Jews also played a role in the city's government. In 1869 Leon Kahn won a seat on the city council and served for eight years. In the 1890s Henry Rauh was also elected to the council.

In the late nineteenth century, Indianapolis Jews were not consigned to a ghetto and forced to live apart from the general population. Instead, they shared in the life of the community. Though Leopold Strauss joined the Americus Club, a social organization for Jewish men, he also belonged to the Maennerchor and Das Deutsche Haus. Strauss identified not only as Jewish but also as German. And his fellow Germans did not exclude him from their organizations because of his Jewish background. Moreover, as Strauss and other German Jews prospered, they moved to residences along fashionable north-side thoroughfares. Indicative of the change, in 1899 the Indianapolis Hebrew Congregation sold their Market Street Temple on the unfashionable near east side and moved to a new site on North Delaware Street. The domain of the Harrisons and their ilk was now home to a synagogue.

By the last decades of the century, a new wave of eastern European Jews was changing the nature of Jewish life in Indianapolis. Less affluent than the north-side Germans, they tended to settle on the south side, where they organized congregations independent of the Indianapolis Hebrew Congregation that served the city's Jewish elite. Polish Jews founded a south-side synagogue in 1870, and Hungarian Jews followed suit, establishing their own congregation in 1884. Russian immigrants founded an additional synagogue in 1889. Whereas the German congregation had embraced Reform Judaism, the south-side Jews remained Orthodox, adhering to traditional religious laws and practices. In 1884 a Russian Jewish newspaper reported on the gap between the Reform Germans and the Orthodox eastern Europeans in Indianapolis. "The Orthodox are Russian and Polish Jews who are strictly Orthodox [and] live, crowded and impoverished, in a small street in the southern part of the city," reported the newspaper. In contrast, the German Reform Jews lived "in ivory towers, in the northern part of the city, in the wealthy section inhabited by the aristocracy."[26] Just as Indianapolis was increasingly divided between the affluent and the less fortunate, so the small Jewish community was not truly a community. The north-side Germans lived a different lifestyle than the poor south-side Poles, Hungarians, and Russians. They shared a Jewish background, but their economic and social positions differed, as did their religious practices.

The Germans, both Jewish and Gentile, were the dominant immigrant group in the city, but Irish newcomers also numbered in the thousands. During the second half of the nineteenth century, the Irish-born population in the city was generally only about half that of the German-born population. This conformed to the prevailing pattern in the Midwest. The Irish were predominant in much of the northeastern United States, and Boston was an Irish city. But they were far less numerous in the Teutonic Midwest.

Less affluent and less skilled than their German-born counterparts, the Irish immigrants were more likely to hold menial jobs. Irish men were employed in construction work, at the railroad yards, and at the Kingan slaughterhouse. Many Irish women became domestic servants. Relatively poor, the Irish newcomers clustered in a near-south-side neighborhood known as Irish Hill located a short distance from the Kingan plant. They generally rallied in support of the Democratic Party. This earned them the enmity of stalwart Republicans, who claimed the Democrats were importing out-of-town Irish voters on election day to guarantee Democrat victory at the polls. In the heated campaign of 1875, a local Republican newspaper denounced the Irish as "villainous-looking cattle," "Hibernian heifers," "Milesian bullocks," and "Romish herds."[27]

Like the Germans, the Irish cemented ties to their fellow compatriots through various organizations. In 1873 the Indianapolis Irish founded a chapter of the Ancient Order of Hibernians and in 1881 organized a lodge of the Friendly Sons of St. Patrick. In 1876 Irish women in Indianapolis established a group known as the Maids of Erin. Irish men also joined a military association called the Emmett Guards. The centers of social life for many Irish were the local Roman Catholic churches. St. John's, St. Patrick's, and Holy Cross served the Irish Hill neighborhood, providing both spiritual and social support for their many parishioners.

Five men of Irish ancestry won the Indianapolis mayor's office in the late nineteenth century. This, however, was no indication of the political power of the Irish Catholic newcomers. Each of the five were Protestants and thus a class apart from the Irish Catholics who inhabited the poor south-side neighborhoods. The only one of these mayors who was actually born in Ireland was the powerful Democrat leader Thomas Taggart. A native of Ulster in the North of Ireland, Taggart and his wife were members of the fashionable St. Paul's Episcopal Church, spiritual home to many of Indianapolis's elite. In Indianapolis there was no Irish Catholic political machine similar to New York City's Tammany Hall. The city's Irish lined up behind the Democratic Party's stance against restrictions on alcohol and its antipathy to expanding rights for African Americans. But Irish Catholics in Indianapolis actually wielded limited political power and did not rival the economic clout of the city's German Americans.

Another group adding to the diversity of Indianapolis was the African Americans. They were not newcomers from abroad but instead migrated in increasing numbers from south of the Ohio River. Like the Germans and Irish, they came to Indianapolis in search of a better life. The growing city offered greater freedom and opportunity for those fleeing the autocratic regimes of Germany, British rule in Ireland, and white oppression and unrewarding agricultural labor in the American South.

Especially notable was the first great migration of Blacks during the 1860s. In 1860, 496 African Americans lived in Indianapolis, making up 2.7 percent of the city's population. Ten years later the number had increased sixfold to 2,931, or 6.1 percent of all Indianapolis residents. In 1880 the figure was 6,504 African Americans, 8.7 percent of the city's total, and in 1900 the count had risen to 15,931, constituting 9.4 percent of Indianapolis's population.

At the turn of the century, African Americans were very much a minority in the city, yet they were a substantial minority compared to Black communities in other northern cities. In 1900 in both Chicago and New York City, Blacks were only 1.8 percent of the population, and the figure for Detroit was 1.4 percent. Cincinnati's Black community represented 4.4 percent of the city's residents; in the former slave state of Missouri, the Black contingent accounted for only 6.2 percent of Saint Louis's population. The racial composition of Indianapolis was not, then, typical of northern American cities. African Americans had a considerably larger presence in the Hoosier capital than in the nation's greatest metropolises. Indianapolis's Black community was unusually significant in numbers; the growing city was not lily white.

As early as 1870, Indiana Avenue, northwest of the city center, was emerging as the hub of Indianapolis's African American community. In 1865 the first Black-owned businesses opened along the avenue, and during the ensuing decades, many others would appear. Just as Fountain Square was developing as a secondary business district for south-side residents, Indiana Avenue would become the center of African American enterprise in the city. It was the place for Indianapolis's Black residents to shop, eat, drink, and enjoy themselves. Indianapolis may have been an improvement over the former slave states of the South, but local Blacks knew that they would not be welcome in many white-owned establishments. Along Indiana Avenue, however, they carved out their own niche, a place where they could live and conduct business relatively free of the dominant white community.

Yet Indianapolis Blacks did not accede passively to white rule; instead, they sought to gain influence and privileges through political action. Consequently, most African Americans lined up loyally behind the Republican Party, which had favored the emancipation of slaves and had secured ratification of the equal protection clause of the Fourteenth Amendment and Black voting rights in the Fifteenth Amendment. By contrast, the Democratic Party was the organ of white supremacy and a seeming threat to Blacks who sought advancement in the Hoosier capital.

Owing to their devotion to the Republican Party, African Americans found themselves at odds with the predominantly Democrat Irish Catholics. Not only were the two groups political rivals, but they also vied for jobs at the bottom of the economic ladder. Both groups were largely confined to menial employment, and a successful Black job seeker might mean unemployment for an Irish immigrant. In 1876 the latent hostility between the two groups erupted into violence. Responding to rumors that Democrats were intimidating Blacks and other Republicans in a special election, about one hundred African Americans from the Fourth Ward marched on the Irish Sixth Ward. Both sides armed themselves with wagon spokes from a local wheelworks, and they attacked their opponents with these clubs, supplemented by bricks, rocks, and eventually revolvers. In the resulting melee, the foes fired at least one hundred shots. Some of the African Americans were wounded by the gunfire, and many endured beatings. One Black man suffered a fatal stab wound. Mayor John Caven intervened and spoke to both sides, urging an end to the violence. The Irish and Blacks retreated, ending the city's most serious racial disturbance of the late nineteenth century.

The African American community's devotion to the Republican Party would pay off for some Black leaders. In 1872 Robert Bagby was elected on the Republican ticket as the first Black member of the city council. African Americans also won seats on the city council in the 1890s, with Henry Sweetland serving from 1890 to 1892 and John A. Puryear from 1892 to 1897. When Puryear stepped down in 1897, his fellow council members honored their departing Black colleague by naming a near-north-side street after him. In 1880 John Hinton was elected on the Republican ticket as the first African American to serve in the Indiana House of Representatives. In 1896 Republican Gabriel Jones also won a house seat, representing Indianapolis African Americans in the state legislature.

Moreover, some Black residents secured positions on the public payroll. In 1876 the city of Indianapolis hired its first contingent of Black firefighters and police officers. At the time few cities in the United States were willing to assign such duties to African Americans. The firefighters were segregated within the force, and Blacks were assigned to the Number Nine Hose Reel House, a unit that was to be staffed solely by Blacks. Yet some public employees were able to rise in the ranks. Benjamin Thornton, born a slave, became one of the first Black police officers in the city, and in 1886 he was promoted to detective, the first African American to achieve that rank.

Indianapolis Republicans realized that the Black community could not be totally ignored. In 1910 Jacob P. Dunn, a journalist and local historian, recognized that African Americans were essential to GOP victories when he wrote, "Very few Republican candidates have received a majority of the white votes of the city since 1880."[28] During the final decades of the nineteenth century, the Indianapolis electorate was fairly evenly divided between Republicans and Democrats. To win, the Republicans had to ensure that African Americans turned out on election day and voted a straight Republican ticket. The Black vote was a key deciding factor in Indianapolis politics.

One African American who prospered in both politics and business was George Knox. He was born a slave but later moved to Indiana, where he learned to be a barber. By the mid-1890s Knox operated a number of barber shops and employed a workforce of fifty. He also became friends with a number of prominent whites, including President Benjamin Harrison, and served as a delegate to the Republican National Conventions of 1892 and 1896. He acquired the *Indianapolis Freeman*, a newspaper serving the African American community, and used it to promote Harrison and the Republican Party.

Knox was not the only African American to publish a newspaper. In 1879 Robert Bagby and his brothers established the *Indianapolis Leader*, the *Colored World* appeared in 1883, and in 1897 the *Indianapolis Recorder* began publication. These were weekly journals that reported news of special interest to their Black readers. Like the German-language press, the African American newspapers testified to the diversity of Indianapolis. Downtown daily newspapers could not serve the special needs of Germans and Blacks, as immigrants and racial minorities wanted coverage of the events most pertinent to them and editorials that addressed their concerns as subgroups within the larger population. The white Anglo-American press did not suffice. The *Leader*, for example, published articles about Black success and editorialized in favor of equal rights and the advancement of the race. For both Germans and African Americans, their newspapers were channels through which they preserved their identity and pursued their interests in a city dominated by English-speaking whites.

Another mainstay of Indianapolis Blacks were their churches. Just as the Roman Catholic churches served as centers for Irish life in the Hoosier capital, Black churches exercised a powerful influence among residents largely segregated from the larger white community. Especially important were the Black Baptist churches, which proliferated as newcomers arrived from south of the Ohio River. By 1900 Indianapolis was home to at least fifteen African American Baptist congregations that offered not only spiritual sustenance for the community but were also a focus of political and social life. For example, Moses Broyles, pastor of the Second Baptist congregation, opened his church to political meetings and supported the Republican Party agenda through his sermons. The Second Baptist Church also provided a less serious social outlet for its parishioners. In the 1870s the Ladies Aid Society of Broyles's church held suppers and festivals as fundraisers for the congregation, feeding the parishioners' stomachs as well as their spirits. Not as numerous but also significant were the city's African Methodist Episcopal churches. Like their Baptist counterparts and the Black press, they provided a cultural niche in which African Americans could satisfy their own needs.

By 1900, then, Indianapolis was a diverse city accommodating residents of widely differing backgrounds. As a growing city, it adjusted to a variety of newcomers and stitched together some semblance of community among sometimes conflicting groups. It included thousands of German speakers as well as those who only knew English. Irish Catholic Democrats clashed with Black Republican Baptists, and Jewish immigrants added a new dimension to the predominantly Christian city. Indianapolis had taken off. It was no longer a relatively homogeneous small town.

Instead, it was a big house with rooms for a multitude of different residents.

LEARNING AND CULTURE

As late nineteenth-century Indianapolis grew in population and prosperity, it acquired the educational and cultural advantages of a major city. German Americans fostered the musical life of the community, introducing supposedly tone-deaf Yankees to the musical heritage of the fatherland. In addition, Indianapolis developed a school system, a public library, literary life, and an art scene, creating a cultural milieu at least equal to that existing in rival midwestern cities. Indianapolis was not only successfully emerging from the mud and isolation of its early years, it was also dispelling cultural desolation and proving to be a city that produced scholars and artists as well as pork and milling machinery.

Essential to the city's intellectual advancement was the development of a system of free public schools. Before the 1850s private schools charging fees provided education to the city's children. Parents paid tuition to the many elementary schools, and private academies or seminaries offered instruction to older youths. In 1852, however, the state legislature authorized localities to levy taxes in support of free public schools, and the following year, the first free schools opened in Indianapolis and a high school was established. The new school system flourished and in 1857 employed thirty-five teachers instructing eighteen hundred students. Then, in 1858, the Indiana Supreme Court struck down the law authorizing cities to levy taxes to fund the salaries of public school teachers, ruling it a violation of the state's constitution. According to a later report of the city's school board, this devastating decision "commenced the dark age of the public schools."[29] The high school closed, and the elementary schools were open for only a few months each year. Following the decision, the *Indiana School Journal* reported, "More than two-thirds of the children of this city are out of school at present." It added,

"A great number of poor private schools have sprung up since the ruin of the public schools."[30]

Conditions gradually improved during the 1860s under the leadership of school superintendent Abraham Shortridge. He reopened the high school and in 1867 organized a training school for teachers. The legislature enacted a new law authorizing cities to levy taxes for salaries, and the state supreme court later upheld it, laying to rest the issue. By 1871 there were nearly 6,500 pupils and 103 teachers in the city's public schools. Indiana, however, had not enacted a compulsory attendance law, and many of Indianapolis's youths remained unschooled.

One group neglected in the 1850s and 1860s was the growing African American population. In 1866, however, the officers of the local school board and Superintendent Shortridge issued an appeal for "The Education of Colored Persons." They noted that "the colored people of the state and city have from the beginning . . . been deprived of advantages from the school fund or any privileges of the schools," and they asked, "If general taxation is for the protection of the community and adds to its wealth and greatness, is not that prosperity lessened by so much as any class are permitted to grow up in ignorance?" They reported that "nearly three hundred are attending private colored pay schools conducted and supported by themselves," which indicated "an earnest desire for improvement." Shortridge and the school board argued that these Black youths should not be denied the benefits of free schools. They concluded, "In our judgment, humanity, justice and sound public policy demand that this class of our citizens shall receive the benefit of our common school system."[31]

Responding to such arguments, the state legislature authorized public schooling for African Americans in 1869. Black pupils were to attend elementary schools segregated by race, unless they lived in an area where there were too few African Americans to warrant a separate Black school. According to Shortridge, by 1874 more than eight hundred African Americans were attending the Indianapolis public schools. There were not enough Black students seeking a secondary education, however, to justify the creation of a separate African American high school. Consequently, in 1872 a delegation headed by Moses Broyles approached Shortridge seeking admission for Black students to the all-white high school. Shortridge responded by escorting a prospective Black student to the high school, where she was admitted and remained without incident until graduation. For the remainder of the nineteenth century, the high school admitted both Blacks and whites, although the city maintained segregated elementary schools.

By the 1880s and 1890s, secondary education in the city was changing. Throughout the United States, there was increased interest in practical, manual education, and German Americans were especially committed to schooling that included classes in architectural drawing, mechanical drafting, and woodworking. In 1888 Indianapolis High School began to offer such courses, and in the early 1890s, the school board constructed an additional high school on the south side that was intended to focus on manual training. This new institution, which became known as Manual High School, actually developed a dual curriculum, offering both academic and vocational courses. In fact, its first principal, Charles Emmerich, taught two courses on the Latin poet Virgil. Manual's two-pronged approach was very popular, and the school attracted a large student body. By 1900, then, Indianapolis had two high schools, Manual on the south side and Indianapolis High School (renamed Shortridge in 1897) on the north side.

Higher education was also available in Indianapolis. In 1850 the state legislature chartered Northwestern Christian University. Founded by members of the Disciples of Christ church, the university, according to its charter, was "to teach and inculcate the Christian faith and Christian morality," as well as provide "for the instruction of the students in every branch of liberal and professional education." When it opened in the mid-1850s, it admitted both men and women on an equal basis, which was relatively uncommon at the time. The state gazetteer of 1858 praised this coeducational scheme as "one of the agencies of securing to woman that broad and liberal development that shall make her not a doll of fashion or an observant of popinjay flatteries, but a *woman*, a *true companion* and *help meet* for man."[32]

The university's chief benefactor was Ovid Butler, a prominent Indianapolis lawyer who drafted the school's charter and donated both the land for its site and much of the endowment. In 1869 Butler funded a chair in English literature, specifying that the chair should always be occupied by a woman. It was the nation's first endowed chair established specifically for a woman. Butler selected Catherine Merrill as the first person to hold the chair. She was the daughter of Samuel Merrill, the state treasurer who, in 1824, had endured the long trek from Corydon to Indianapolis. Having taught in private schools for many years, Catherine Merrill was one of the most respected educators in the city. Recognizing Ovid Butler's long-term devotion to Northwestern Christian, in 1877 the board of trustees renamed it Butler University.

Further enhancing Indianapolis's intellectual credentials was the establishment of a well-respected public library. Prior to the Civil War, no free circulating public library existed in the city. There had been subscription libraries funded by fees charged to readers. A small collection of dog-eared books in a cupboard in the township trustees' office constituted the township library. The largest number of books was in the state library housed in the capitol. This library was created for the benefit of legislators and state officials. It included volumes of public documents and tomes useful to lawmakers, but it had few novels or popular works. Moreover, the general public could not borrow works from the collection but could only use them in the statehouse reading room.

Dedicated to serving his students and the reading public generally, Superintendent Shortridge mobilized the school board and proposed legislation for a tax to fund free circulating libraries. In 1871 the state legislature accepted Shortridge's proposal and authorized such a levy. Two years later the Indianapolis

Public Library opened with a collection of 14,560 books under the supervision of Charles Evans, a professionally trained librarian imported from the East Coast. It proved a success. During the first year of operation, 5,220 borrowers registered, approximately one-tenth of the city's population. By comparison, 4,410 registered at Cincinnati's public library, and the figure for the much larger city of Boston was 6,688. Indianapolis borrowers took out more than 100,000 volumes during the first year of operation. In his first annual report, Evans emphasized the importance of the library in the growing city's development. "The opening of the library has awakened many to the fact that the intellectual growth of the city should keep pace with the material growth," he observed. "They should go hand in hand to make the name of the city, not only the synonym for wealth and great business activity; but also for a large and liberal culture."[33] The library was deemed an integral element of Indianapolis's escape from small-town status. Indianapolis was an emerging material success, and to prove its new significance, it had to establish its intellectual credentials as well. The library would prove that Indianapolis was not an inferior backwater but a city that would eventually rank with Cincinnati and Boston.

During the remaining years of the century, the public library grew in volumes and circulation. By 1883 it included 35,000 volumes and recorded a circulation of 195,000. To reach the city's expanding neighborhoods, in 1896 the library established four branch facilities, the first of many additional branches opened in the coming decades. With a growing collection and an increasing number of borrowers, the Indianapolis Public Library was realizing the aspirations of Shortridge and Evans.

In his first annual report, Evans also noted "the increased literary activity in the city." According to the librarian, "Never before have the number of 'reading clubs' and social meetings for the discussion of literary topics been so numerous."[34] Evans was not mistaken. Over the following two decades, literary societies proliferated in the city as Indianapolis residents embraced literature and the pursuit of culture. In 1875 local women founded the Indianapolis Woman's Club focusing on the domestic and intellectual life of its members. Though not exclusively devoted to literature, the Woman's Club developed into a force dedicated to the advancement of higher culture in the Hoosier capital. In 1877 a group of men, including librarian Charles Evans, formed the Indianapolis Literary Club. Its constitution specified, "The object of this club shall be social, literary and aesthetic culture."[35] At the meetings a member would deliver a paper on a "literary or aesthetic" topic, and discussion would ensue. It was a decidedly elite conclave, and its members included some of the city's most prominent citizens, such as poet James Whitcomb Riley and President Benjamin Harrison.

Another elite north-side society was the Fortnightly Literary Club, a women's group founded in 1885. Its first president was Cornelia Cole Fairbanks, wife of a future vice president of the United States. Each meeting included the presentation of a paper written by one of the members followed by conversation. Among the essays presented in 1885–1886 were "George Eliot," "Victor Hugo's Works," and "Does Goethe Rank the Peer of Shakespeare?" But the topics were not always strictly literary and included "Housekeeping in the Nineteenth Century," "Florida, Past and Present," and "Women Prominent as Philanthropists."[36] As in the case of the other literary clubs, *literary* was conceived broadly as meaning anything contributing to the intellectual uplift of the members and the larger community.

Membership in literary clubs was not, however, restricted to only a select few. Instead, there were intellectual organizations for a broad range of Indianapolis residents. Jews formed the Agiliar Literary Society, and African Americans organized the Garnett Literary Society in 1883, opening it to both men and women. Other African American literary groups were the Parlor Reading Circle and the Douglass Literary Society. The Deutsche-Literarischer Klub (German Literary Club) was a natural addition to the list in the bilingual Hoosier capital. It included both German American and Anglo-American women interested in German literature and culture in general. The club required that all papers and discussion be in the German language. Use of English was forbidden.

In 1888 the Indianapolis Woman's Club took the lead in providing a home for the various women's cultural groups proliferating in the city. The club formed a stock company to erect a building, known as the Propylaeum, to serve as a meeting place. According to the Propylaeum's articles of association, the building was to be used for "literary, artistic, scientific, industrial, musical, mechanical and education purposes" and would particularly accommodate women's groups.[37] It did not remain exclusively a female domain, as the male Indianapolis Literary Club met there for a time. *Propylaeum* was Greek for gateway or passage, and the new gathering place served as one of the city's prime gateways to culture. It was a structure that marked the community's passage into big-city status, intellectually as well as materially.

Indianapolis residents were not only reading literature at the public library and discussing it at the Propylaeum, some were also creating works that appealed to readers nationwide. The most notable figure was James Whitcomb Riley, who published his first book of verse in 1883 and remained a popular poet and revered local citizen until his death in 1916. He both wrote and performed, traveling the lecture circuit and delighting audiences with readings of his poems and humorous anecdotes. By the close of the century, younger Indianapolis authors were also attracting attention. In 1899 Booth Tarkington's first novel, *The Gentleman from Indiana*, appeared, and in 1900 Meredith Nicholson's *The Hoosiers* was published. Both men would go on to greater achievements, with Tarkington winning two Pulitzer Prices in the early twentieth century. Both also would remain in Indianapolis, as would Riley. At the close of the nineteenth century, the best young Indianapolis writers were not boarding trains for the literary centers of New York or Boston and abandoning the supposed cultural wasteland of a midwestern factory and railroad town. One did not need to leave Indianapolis for the East Coast to achieve literary recognition. Instead, emerging authors could find fame, fortune, and inspiration in their midwestern hometown.

One sign of Indianapolis's emerging cultural maturity was the success of the Bowen-Merrill publishing firm. This Indianapolis-based company published thirty of the thirty-nine works by Riley that were brought out during his lifetime. Both the Indianapolis publisher and the poet profited handsomely, and this success earned Bowen-Merrill national recognition.

At the close of the century, Bowen-Merrill proved that Riley was not its only asset. In 1898 it published Charles Major's *When Knighthood Was in Flower*, which was a bestseller, rising to second place in sales among American books. In 1900 three of the top-ten sellers were Bowen-Merrill imprints, and that same year, the Indianapolis publisher brought out its first children's book, L. Frank Baum's *The Wonderful Wizard of Oz*. By the turn of the century, Indianapolis's emergence as a publishing center distinguished it from other inland American cities. American publishing was increasingly concentrated in New York City. Yet Bowen-Merrill defied New York's dominance, bringing out bestsellers read throughout the United States.

Meanwhile, the visual arts were flourishing in Indianapolis. From 1850 to 1880, a number of painters had created portraits and landscapes for the local market, but efforts to advance the visual arts had faltered. In 1856 the Indianapolis Art Society was founded, but its existence was short lived. Painters John Love and James F. Gookins opened the Indiana Art School in 1877. It initially attracted a number of students, but the enterprise folded after two years. There did not seem to be enough interest in art to sustain viable organizations or schools.

Undeterred, in May 1883, May Wright Sewall invited a group of women to gather in her parlor and consider the creation of a society for the promotion and study of art. Sewall was a dynamic presence in the cultural life of the city. As a leader of the Indianapolis Woman's Club, she was largely responsible for the building of the Propylaeum. A ubiquitous figure, the Anglo-American Sewall even became a member of the German Literary

Society. If anyone could create a permanent art association in the Hoosier capital, she could.

On April 5, 1883, Sewall and seventeen other women signed an article of association that stated the purpose of their new art association: "To cultivate and advance Art in all its branches, to provide means for instruction in the various branches of Art; to establish for that end a permanent gallery, and to establish and produce lectures upon subjects relevant to Art."[38] In October the organization was incorporated as the Art Association of Indianapolis, and it presented its first exhibition one month later. Local artist Susan Ketcham, traveling to Chicago, Detroit, and New York, gathered a collection of 453 paintings by 137 artists for this successful first show. The Art Association of Indianapolis opened a school in 1884, but it proved a financial failure and closed after two years. The association's annual shows survived, however, and became one of the mainstays of the city's cultural life during the remainder of the century.

In 1885 the annual exhibition was devoted to "The Hoosier Colony in München," focusing on the works of Theodore C. Steele and William Forsyth, who were studying art at the Royal Academy in the Bavarian capital. Steele and Forsyth later became leading figures in the city's art life and attracted supporters beyond the local scene. In 1894 they, together with Richard Gruelle, Otto Stark, and John Ottis Adams, exhibited in Chicago, winning praise from Windy City art lovers. The novelist Hamlin Garland dubbed them "the Hoosier group," a label that would distinguish them among devotees of art for decades to come.

In 1890 Mary Steele, wife of Theodore C. Steele, sought to further artistic endeavor in the city by founding the Portfolio Club. It was similar to the literary societies; at each meeting a member read a paper on a subject related to art, discussion ensued, and a musical performance followed. For example, in October 1895, Otto Stark, who had studied in Paris, delivered a paper on "Art Students' Life in Paris," and in April 1896, Richard Lieber, art critic for the *Indianapolis Journal* and member of a prominent German American family, spoke on Germany.

One of the members of the Portfolio Club was Joseph Bowles, who enlivened the local art scene through publication of the periodical *Modern Art*. A fervent disciple of William Morris, the progenitor of the British arts and crafts movement, Bowles sought to apply the movement's principles to his journal. Morris and his followers believed that all creations, including furniture, wallpaper, textiles, ceramics, silver, and publications, should be works of art, conforming to the highest principles of design. Rebelling against the mass machine production of utilitarian objects, the British reformer advocated the making of handcrafted works of beauty that would raise the aesthetic standards of the industrializing world. In accord with this belief, Bowles intended his quarterly to be a work of art as well as a work about art. Local designer and illustrator Bruce Rogers embellished the issues, which included articles by Steele and Gruelle, among others. Congratulating Bowles, Hamlin Garland wrote, "Your beautiful magazine is a wonderfully fine output, perilously fine."[39] Though it never enjoyed a mass circulation, Bowles's journal was sold in bookstores in sixteen cities in the United States as well as in London, Paris, Leipzig, and Florence.

Bowles began publication in 1893, but because of a change of ownership, Bowles and his journal moved to Boston in 1895. For those two years, however, Indianapolis was on the cutting edge of the art world. From the heart of Indiana, Bowles promoted the influential arts and crafts movement that was sweeping the world, and *Modern Art* published Steele's observations on French impressionism when the likes of Monet and Renoir were deemed avant-garde in the United States.

Bowles was not the only one in Indianapolis drawn to the international arts and crafts movement. In 1898 devotees of handcrafted artifacts organized an arts and crafts exhibition at the newly renamed Shortridge High School. This proved so successful that a second show was held the following year. Two thousand people attended the opening reception in 1899. According to the *Indianapolis News*, the exhibition included "paintings in oil and water color, sketches in ink, pencil and pastel, examples of book-making, wood carving, ceramics, engraving, etching, art glass, grilles, miniatures, plastic decorations, tile, terra cotta, photography . . . wrought iron, embroidery, and lace." Gruelle proclaimed, "Here beauty vies with beauty, whether in the time-defying terra cotta or wrought-iron or the most delicate and dainty fabrications of lace and embroidery, all being a messenger of beauty and usefulness, all go toward uplifting and making the world better, . . . all tend toward making our city truly beautiful in the eyes of the world."[40]

Further adding to the artistic euphoria of Indianapolis in the 1890s was the fortuitous bequest of John Herron. Upon his death in 1895, Herron left the bulk of his estate to the Art Association of Indianapolis. Although it had struggled financially since its founding, the association now had the funds to fulfill its aspirations. During the first decade of the twentieth century, the association opened an art school and art museum and joined the growing number of American cities with a permanent art collection on display for the enjoyment and edification of the local populace.

At the close of the century, then, Indianapolis could boast of a cultural future as promising as its commercial fortunes. In 1899 Wilhelmina Seegmiller, the director of art education in the Indianapolis public schools, quoted a local businessman who proclaimed, "The conditions in Indianapolis are ripe for a renaissance in art. The feeling of the people is similar to that of the people of Florence at the beginning of the Renaissance." According to this enthusiast, "Every one, from the street-car driver to the wealthiest business man, is taking an active interest in the development of art." Though one might dismiss this as hyperbole, Seegmiller took it seriously enough to repeat it and recognize "much truth in the statement."[41] With money in the coffers of the Art Association, a body of craftspeople creating everything from lace to wrought iron grills, and the Hoosier group artists producing works inspired by the beauties of the Indiana landscape, local optimists believed that Indianapolis was poised for artistic greatness.

In 1897, in a speech before the Commercial Club, former president Benjamin Harrison spoke of the city's status as a major city. Referring to the biblical passage where the Apostle Paul claimed that as a native of Tarsus, he was a citizen of "no mean city," Harrison proceeded to extol Indianapolis as likewise no mean city. In the Roman world of Paul, Tarsus was not an obscure or insignificant city, and similarly in the United States of 1897, Indianapolis was no longer a backwater but had risen to a position of distinction. The former president quipped, "That Indianapolis is not an Indian reservation with a classical termination is now generally known in the Eastern states and also by some of our English kin."[42] Indianapolis, like ancient Tarsus, was known for its excellent schools and as a transportation center. Indianapolis needed to continue to strive to become an ideal community, but in the minds of Harrison and his listeners, it was decidedly no mean city. Over the course of five decades, it had taken off and emerged as a city known even to short-sighted provincials on the East Coast and in England.

3

Reaching Maturity
1900–1945

In June 1920 Indianapolis marked its one-hundredth birthday with five days of celebrations. The festivities began with a mass meeting featuring commemorative speeches on day one, followed on the second day by a musical extravaganza including a four-hundred-person choir and a performance by the Cincinnati Symphony Orchestra. The prime attraction on day three was a parade of 122 floats and fourteen bands, with nearly half the city's population lining the parade route. Highlighting day four was a pageant depicting the history of Indianapolis. In a stirring finale, its cast of nearly two thousand local residents joined in singing "Glory, glory, Hallelujah! In-di-an-ap-o-lis!" to the tune of the "Battle Hymn of the Republic." On day five, fireworks and a band concert concluded the festivities. The city was one hundred years old, and its residents exuberantly proclaimed its progress from wilderness settlement to major metropolis. Indianapolis had reached full maturity, and in the minds of many of its residents, the century-old city deserved a gala party.

At one hundred years, Indianapolis had achieved its destiny and fully established itself in the galaxy of urban America. In the federal censuses from 1900 to 1940, it ranked twentieth, twenty-first, or twenty-second in population among American cities. Its development relative to the nation as a whole had plateaued. The Hoosier capital was no longer a boomtown soaring past rivals, as was the case from 1850 to 1880. Yet it was not a declining city, falling behind the nation's pack. Instead, it continued to grow and maintain its relative position. Indianapolis would not join the ranks of New York City, Chicago, and Philadelphia as one of nation's urban giants. Nor was it rising dramatically in the ranks like the new boomtowns of Los Angeles, Dallas, Houston, and Miami. Its twentieth-century destiny was to remain the unchallenged urban hub of Indiana and a city secure in its place as a second-tier American metropolis.

THE MOBILE CITY

On January 1, 1900, the first electric intercity railroad car arrived in Indianapolis, having completed the twelve-mile trip from Greenwood, Indiana. This marked another advance in Indianapolis's history as a transportation center and the crossroads of America. The electric interurbans would further increase traffic to the city and make Indianapolis more accessible than ever. The number of lines proliferated rapidly, and by 1910 twelve companies operated interurban cars linking Indianapolis to cities throughout Indiana and beyond. In 1914 the Indiana Public Service Commission reported, "It is with pride that we here note that the city of Indianapolis is the center of the largest and most important interurban development in the United States."[1]

Like city streetcars, interurbans were electric railroads, but as the name implied, they ran between cities rather than simply transporting passengers within a single municipality. They charged cheaper fares than the steam railroads and offered more frequent service. In addition, the interurbans made more stops, picking up passengers at country crossroads as well as in cities. Basically, they provided service comparable to streetcars, furnishing inexpensive and convenient transit from small towns and rural areas to Indiana's largest city.

In 1904 the Indianapolis Traction Terminal opened as a common depot for the many interurban lines converging on the city. Located halfway between the statehouse and Monument Circle, the terminal was at the very heart of Indianapolis. It included a nine-track train shed as well as a nine-story office building that housed most of the offices of the traction companies. It also provided a waiting room, ticket offices, a restaurant, and a newsstand for interurban travelers. The terminal was a full-service depot designed to accommodate the rapidly expanding interurban industry. In 1906 it served 4,469,950 passengers; by 1916 the number of passengers passing through the terminal had risen to 7,208,747 transported by 462 trains daily. It boasted of being the greatest interurban terminal in the world.

The web of interurban lines markedly enhanced the mobility of Hoosiers. Residents from outlying towns and farms could readily access Indianapolis and enjoy the shopping and entertainment options of the big city. Arriving at the Traction Terminal in the heart of the city, passengers could transact their business and easily return home in time for dinner. The interurbans provided the advantages of life in Indianapolis to residents from throughout much of the state.

By 1920, however, the interurbans were facing serious competition from the burgeoning number of automobiles. Motor vehicles were luring passengers from the lines and contributed to the decline and ultimate doom of the interurbans in the 1920s and 1930s. Yet the eclipse of the interurbans did not spell an end to Indianapolis's role in the history of American mobility. Just as the Hoosier capital was a center of interurban development, it also played a key role in automotive history. By the time of Indianapolis's centennial in 1920, the city had acquired a worldwide reputation for automotive speed.

In the early 1890s, carriage maker Charles Black assembled the first automobile in Indianapolis and drove it through the city streets to the amazement of the local citizenry. Black claimed to have built the first automobile in the United States, though there were other claimants to this distinction. During the 1890s a number of mechanically minded tinkerers were building motor vehicles, but by the close of the decade, horseless carriages were still a rare sight on city streets, and automaking was in its infancy.

Traction Terminal

In 1898 the Waverly Company became the first Indianapolis firm that could actually claim to be a manufacturer of automobiles. It produced an electric car powered by a battery. In 1900 the National Automobile and Electric Company also turned out an electric vehicle with 2.5 horsepower and a maximum speed of fifteen miles per hour. As of June 1900, this small-time Indianapolis manufacturer employed forty workers.

Over the following decade, the number of automakers in Indianapolis increased rapidly as eager entrepreneurs sought to profit from the growing fascination with motor vehicles. Some established Indianapolis manufacturers were among those drawn to the new industry. In 1905 Howard Marmon of the Nordyke and Marmon milling machinery company began commercial production of the Marmon automobile. Advertised as "A Mechanical Masterpiece," the Marmon was a high-priced vehicle appealing to a clientele who could afford its vaunted reliability and comfort. Carriage maker David Parry likewise decided it was time to cash in on the growing demand for automobiles. In 1905 he purchased control of the Overland Auto Company and moved its operations from Terre Haute, Indiana, to Indianapolis. A new owner later moved Overland production to Toledo, but in 1909 the carriage builder established the Parry Auto Company, which for a few years produced the appropriately named Parry.

Other manufacturers created their own brands during the first decade of the century. The National company reorganized and, under the leadership of Arthur Newby, produced gasoline-fueled motorcars. Like the Marmon, the National was an expensive vehicle known for its high-quality construction. In 1909 local carriage maker Joseph Cole founded the Cole Motor Car Company, producer of another luxury vehicle. The Cole company survived until 1925 and over its sixteen years of existence turned out 40,717 cars.

By 1912 Indianapolis was home to twelve automakers. The city's seven thousand autoworkers produced an estimated 10,300 vehicles annually. The focus, however, was on quality rather than quantity. Indianapolis cars were generally in the medium or high price range, with an average sales tag of $2,000. The *Indianapolis Star* observed that locally made autos were "characterized by good material and careful and honest workmanship." According to the newspaper, "there is no attempt at wholesale flooding of the country by sacrificing quality to quantity."[2]

The much-vaunted quality and craftsmanship of Indianapolis would seriously limit the city's future as an automaker. For a time in the early twentieth century, Indianapolis seemed poised to rival Detroit as the nation's motorcar capital. Yet Detroit manufacturers, most notably Henry Ford, realized that the American consumer wanted quantity as well as quality. Moreover, millions of prospective car buyers could not afford a Marmon. Only through mass production could automakers meet consumer demand and turn out reasonably priced vehicles. Detroit excelled at that. Indianapolis did not. In 1916 Henry Ford's plants produced five hundred thousand autos selling for $345 each. This was twelve times the total sixteen-year production of Cole, one of Indianapolis's most successful brands. During the second decade of the twentieth century, Indianapolis fell out of the running as an automaker. Detroit, not Indianapolis, was to be the Motor City.

The Hoosier capital did, however, continue to make high-quality vehicles admired by car aficionados. In 1913 Harry Stutz organized the Stutz Motor Car Company, which produced 2,200 automobiles in 1917. Its famed Stutz Bearcat was a sporty vehicle known for its speed. Everyone had heard of the Bearcat, but relatively few could afford one. American car enthusiasts might dream of a Stutz Bearcat, but most had to settle for a Model T Ford. In 1920 the brothers Fred and August Duesenberg opened an auto plant in Indianapolis, producing an exemplary automobile bearing their name. The Duesenberg was to be the most expensive car ever produced in the United States. Experts agreed that the magnificent motor vehicle was worth its awesome price tag, yet that did not translate into mass sales. The Duesenberg was a grand creation rather than a practical vehicle for transporting the average American to work or to the store.

Actually, Indianapolis did benefit from Ford's success as a mass-producer of automobiles. As sales of the Model T soared, Henry Ford decided to open branch assembly plants that would build the finished automobile from parts and chassis manufactured in Detroit. In 1914 Ford built a regional assembly plant in Indianapolis that was turning out more than twenty-five thousand Model Ts annually by the early 1920s. In terms of the number of automobiles produced, Indianapolis was more significant as an adjunct to Detroit than as a competitor. Indianapolis produced fine automobiles, but Detroit surged ahead in production, profits, and population.

As a maker of automotive parts, Indianapolis also earned a place in motor vehicle history. Carl Fisher and James Allison organized the Prest-O-Lite company, which manufactured acetylene-powered headlights for early automobiles. Prest-O-Lite proved a great success. Equipped with the company's headlights, the growing army of auto owners could enjoy motoring at night as well as in the daytime. Fisher and Allison began their business with a $2,000 investment. In 1917 they sold it to Union Carbide for $9 million. Another major automotive parts manufacturer was the Wheeler-Schebler Company, maker of carburetors for gasoline-powered engines. Like Prest-O-Lite, Wheeler-Schebler became a major player in the automotive industry and expanded into the production of ignition-system components. Testifying to the financial success of founder Frank Wheeler was his magnificent villa on a thirty-acre estate adjacent to the mansions of the newly enriched Carl Fisher and James Allison.

The advent of the automobile not only made money for a fortunate few but also necessitated the construction of improved highways and the adoption of new regulations. During the second decade of the twentieth century, Carl Fisher was the principal promoter of the Lincoln Highway, a coast-to-coast paved motorway that passed through northern Indiana. He also was the instigator of the Dixie Highway project, which was intended to provide first-rate roadways from the Midwest through the South to Florida. Though Fisher's highways facilitated high-speed travel, Indiana lawmakers were vigilant in restricting speedsters in the state's cities. Reacting to the threat from reckless motorists, the Indiana legislature enacted speed limits in 1905. The maximum permissible speed in business districts and densely populated urban areas was eight miles per hour. In other parts of the city, one could cruise at fifteen miles per hour. In 1913 Hoosier lawmakers raised the limit to ten miles per hour in business districts and maintained a fifteen-mile-per-hour limit in residential areas.

Indianapolis, however, was not to be known for its limits on speed but instead for the unlimited speeds on its raceway. Detroit surpassed Indianapolis in the production of automobiles, but no city would rival the Hoosier capital as a mecca for automobile racing. The name Detroit became synonymous with automobile manufacturing, while the name Indianapolis conjured up thoughts of fast cars on a world-famous speedway. On the final weekend in May each year, Indianapolis became the mass destination for racing fans who filled the city's hotels and restaurants and generated an income that in part compensated for the city's failure to match the success of Henry Ford or General Motors.

The principal figure in the rise of Indianapolis as a racing mecca was Carl Fisher. An entrepreneur and promoter par excellence, Fisher founded Prest-O-Lite, guided the construction of the Lincoln and Dixie Highways, and became the developer of Miami Beach. He was a dynamo who dreamed big and to a remarkable degree achieved his dreams. He raced bicycles in the 1890s, and during the early years of the new century, he was a record-setting driver in automobile races. Having witnessed auto racing in Europe, Fisher concluded that European-made cars were superior to their American counterparts in design, durability, and handling. Concerned about this gap in quality, he proposed creating a track for the testing of American automobiles and for racing contests. Fisher told American carmakers, "The only way to gain the public's confidence quickly is to prove the dependability of your products on the race track."[3] Through high-speed driving on a track, manufacturers would be able to identify the weaknesses in their automobiles and act to bring them up to European standards.

In 1908 Fisher convinced his Prest-O-Lite partner, James Allison, as well as National automaker Arthur Newby and carburetor manufacturer Frank Wheeler, to join him in the purchase of land five miles west of Indianapolis as the site for a track superior to anything then existing in the United States. They incorporated as the Indianapolis Motor Speedway Company in March 1909. Construction began on the two-and-a-half-mile oval raceway that same month, and by August 1909, the Speedway appeared ready for racing.

The track surface of crushed rock and tar, however, proved a tragic liability. During the opening three days of racing, the poor condition of the track was blamed for the deaths of one driver, two riding mechanics, and two spectators. Cars spun out of control after hitting chuckholes, and flying pieces of gravel smashed against the googles of some drivers. Famed race car driver Louis Chevrolet was temporarily blinded. On the third day, officials halted the final race, unwilling to continue what some deemed a bloodbath.

Out-of-town newspapers lambasted the Speedway and called for an end to Fisher's dream, which had seemingly become a nightmare. The *Detroit News* editorialized, "The blood of the Indianapolis Motor Speedway has probably rung the knell on track racing in the United States." The *New York Times* headed its editorial "Slaughter as Spectacle" and argued that auto racing brought "out the very worst of human nature by providing a most barbarous form of excitement." According to the *Times*, the races were "an amusement congenial only to savages and should be stopped." A Syracuse, New York, newspaper proposed that the city of Indianapolis "close up the Speedway and make a skating rink out of it." Some local boosters were more forgiving. The general manager of the L. S. Ayres department store noted an increase in sales during the three-day event, a fact that in part compensated for the deaths. Howard Marmon wrote a long letter headlined "In Defense of Speedway" in a weekly auto periodical. Writing of Indianapolis, another commented, "We have no lakes and no rivers, but we have our railroads and our Speedway . . . what better advertising could be had?"[4]

Undeterred by the bad press, Fisher and his partners set to work to resurface the track. In a short two-month period, the Speedway Company resurfaced the entire raceway with paving bricks. Yet attendance at the 1910 season meets was disappointing. In an attempt to revive interest and draw larger crowds, the management decided to host a single-day racing extravaganza featuring the nation's best drivers vying for what was then a huge purse of $25,000. The result was the first Indianapolis 500-Mile Race.

This time Fisher and his partners were not disappointed. In May 1911 the public responded with enthusiasm, flocking to the Speedway for the much-ballyhooed contest. Hotels were booked solidly, restaurants ran out of food, and the city streets were jammed with visitors heading for the Speedway. Fifteen special trains transported an estimated twelve thousand out-of-town attendees, and interurban lines carried 2,400 people per hour to the downtown Traction Terminal. "Never before in its history has the city entertained a larger throng. Never has there been a more cosmopolitan crowd," proclaimed the *Indianapolis News*. The *News* also reported on the melee on rail lines headed for the Speedway. Some racing enthusiasts who were "fearful of failure to get on board because of the dense throngs around the steps of every car occasionally clambered into trains through open side windows."[5] With a bit of condescension, the *New York Times* observed, "This is the first time that Indianapolis has been over-taxed."[6] In all, an estimated eighty thousand people witnessed the first running of the Indianapolis 500.

Forty cars participated in the initial race, which was won by Ray Harroun piloting an Indianapolis-manufactured Marmon Wasp. He completed the five hundred miles in six hours and forty-two minutes, with an average speed of 74.59 miles per hour. Encouraged by the success of the first Indianapolis 500 race, the Speedway Company doubled the purse for the 1912 running to $50,000. The winner was Joe Dawson at the wheel of an Indianapolis-made National. The first two races not only proved that Indianapolis could become a destination for thousands of people seeking exciting entertainment, they also demonstrated the superiority of Indianapolis vehicles. Locally manufactured motorcars had proved to be the best on the track.

Fortunately, the new brick pavement proved less hazardous than the original surface, and the death rate at the Speedway declined. In the initial Indianapolis 500 race, there was only one

Indianapolis Speedway, 1916

fatality, and there were no further deaths in the Indianapolis 500 races until 1919, when three participants were killed. Auto racing remained a dangerous occupation, but the Speedway never again matched the bloodbath of 1909.

In the Indianapolis 500 races following 1912, Indianapolis automakers could no longer claim victory. In 1913, 1914, 1915, and 1916, European drivers piloting European cars won the race, seemingly confirming Fisher's belief that European vehicles were superior to their American counterparts. Indianapolis-made Duesenbergs won the race in the mid-1920s, but by that time, Indianapolis was largely out of contention as an automobile manufacturer. Instead, its destiny was to be a city famed for auto racing. Each year during the final weekend in May, Indianapolis was to be happily overtaxed as thousands of money-spending visitors converged on the famous city of speed.

DIVERSITY AND DIVISION

During the first decade of the twentieth century, the United States experienced the largest influx of European immigrants in the nation's history. Yet in Indianapolis the foreign-born share of the population continued to decline, dropping from 10.1 percent in 1900 to 8.5 percent in 1910 and 5.4 percent by 1920. This was markedly different from the demographic composition of many of the largest cities in the northern United States. In Chicago the percentage of foreign born rose from 34.6 percent in 1900 to 35.9 percent in 1910, in New York City the increase was from 37.0 percent to 40.8 percent, and in Cleveland the figures for 1900 and 1910 were 32.6 percent and 35.0 percent respectively. Much of urban America was becoming more diverse, receiving a flood of newcomers from abroad. Indianapolis, in contrast, was continuing to build its reputation as a city composed overwhelmingly of native-born Americans.

Some newcomers from Europe did arrive in modest numbers, adding to Indianapolis's diversity. Beginning in the 1890s, Slovenians moved to the Haughville area to work for National Malleable Casting Company and at the Kingan packing plant. During the first decade of the twentieth century, they founded fraternal lodges that offered social support for newcomers in the alien city. Dissatisfied with the local Irish American priest, they secured permission from the Roman Catholic bishop in 1906 to organize their own Slovenian parish presided over by a Slovenian-speaking pastor. The Slovenian community was, however, a minor element in the city. By the onset of World War I, there were only approximately 1,200 Slovenians in Indianapolis.

Another minor Slavic group in Indianapolis were the Bulgarians/Macedonians. Like the Slovenians, they were relegated to low-paying jobs at the National Malleable and Kingan plants. A 1916 study of immigrants in Indianapolis reported that these south Slavic newcomers were largely "housed in a row of three roomed tenements, which [were] without any paint and near the point of disintegration." They lived "under the most unsanitary conditions."[7] American landlords took advantage of the immigrants' need to cluster near the Kingan slaughterhouse, charging rents that were at least 40 percent higher than those for comparable dwellings elsewhere in Indianapolis. The neighborhood housing these immigrants was generally deemed the worst in the city. In 1915 the Bulgarians/Macedonians founded their own Bulgarian Orthodox parish, adding to the religious diversity of the city. Yet, as in the case of the Slovenians, they constituted a small fraction of the city's population, with perhaps 1,100 potential parishioners.

Meanwhile, other nationalities were arriving in small numbers. By 1910 there were 1,137 Italians in Indianapolis, many of them working as fruit and vegetable peddlers. There were small Hungarian and Polish communities and a minor contingent from Serbia. None of these immigrant groups was a major presence in the Hoosier capital comparable to the German newcomers of the nineteenth century. In 1910 Indianapolis remained a largely native-born American city with German overtones.

With the onset of World War I, however, even the German influence would wane. In August 1914 hostilities broke out between the Allied nations of Britain, France, and Russia and the Central Powers of Germany and Austria-Hungary. During the early years of the war, while the United States remained neutral, Indianapolis's German population dedicated themselves to defending their fatherland from British-inspired propaganda. The *Telegraph und Tribuene*, Indianapolis's German-language daily newspaper, carried stories emphasizing German military successes and attacked those Americans who seemed dedicated to drawing the United States into the British-French camp. When President Woodrow Wilson threatened to break off diplomatic relations with Germany because of Germany's submarine warfare, prominent German American business leaders in Indianapolis sent a letter to Indiana senator John Kern urging him to use his influence to prevent a diplomatic break. The Indianapolis German-American Alliance forwarded approximately three hundred to four hundred telegrams to congressmen with the same message. From

Italian fruit vendors

1914 through 1916, Indianapolis's German American community was adamant about keeping the United States from entering the war against Germany and dedicated to forestalling British efforts to lure America into Allied arms.

When the United States entered the war on the side of Britain and France in 1917, the local German community loyally changed its tune. Indiana's governor appointed Richard Lieber, a prominent German native from Indianapolis, as his military secretary with the title of colonel, and Lieber was to rally German American support for the crusade against the kaiser and his minions. One hundred twenty-four members of the Indianapolis turnverein enlisted in the American armed forces. In a competition among local churches to sell war bonds, the German Trinity Lutheran Church placed second, demonstrating that its parishioners were unassailably American patriots and loyal supporter of the Allied cause.

Yet as war fever increased, everything associated with Germany, German culture, or the German language became suspect. The *Telegraph und Tribuene* ceased publication in 1918, unable to perpetuate German-language reporting in a nation dedicated to defeating the German Empire. Das Deutsche Haus changed its name to the less offensive Athenaeum, and the Maennerchor temporarily became the Academy of Music. Bismarck Street, named for the famed German chancellor, became Pershing Street in honor of the American military commander. Another casualty was the German Literary Club, which ceased to exist in 1917. In January 1918 the Indianapolis school board decided to terminate German language instruction in the elementary schools, contending that "the public school should teach our boys and girls the principle of one nation, one language, and one flag, and should not assist in perpetuating the language of an alien enemy in our homes and enemy viewpoints in the community."[8] Then, in 1919, the Indiana legislature outlawed the teaching of German in any school in the state. By the close of the war, it was foolhardy to use the tongue of the fatherland within earshot of any loyal native-born American. Commenting on this difficult time, in 1926 a publication of the Indianapolis turnverein bitterly recalled, "In Indianapolis hatred against the citizens of German extraction was artificially stimulated, and irresponsible hotheads even went so far as to threaten the societies composed of such of their fellow citizens."[9]

The famed novelist Kurt Vonnegut Jr. wrote of the consequences of the anti-German onslaught. A member of one of Indianapolis's most prominent German families, Vonnegut observed, "The anti-Germanism in this country during the First World War so shamed and dismayed my parents that they resolved to raise me without acquainting me with the language or the literature or the music or the oral family histories which my ancestors had loved. They volunteered to make me ignorant and rootless as proof of their patriotism." According to Vonnegut, "This was done with surprising meekness by many, many, German-American families in Indianapolis"; some seemed almost "to boast of this dismantling and quiet burial of a culture."[10] In a few short years, Indianapolis wiped clean its immigrant past. Prevailing opinion seemed to demand that German roots were best forgotten. Instead, the young scions of German families, like Vonnegut, were to grow up unalloyed Americans.

Whereas World War I diminished German culture in Indianapolis, it increased the presence of African Americans. Blacks continued to migrate to Indianapolis throughout the early twentieth century, but the influx of newcomers from the South was especially marked during the wartime decade. Between 1910 and 1920, the city's Black population soared 59 percent from 21,800 to 34,700. By 1920 Blacks constituted one-ninth of the city's population. This was the period of the Great Migration, when African Americans moved to northern cities in unprecedented numbers. World War I disrupted the supply of cheap immigrant labor coming from Europe, and the American South became an alternate source of workers for labor-hungry northern cities. Actually, the migration to Indianapolis was modest compared with the rise in some other midwestern cities. In Chicago the Black population more than doubled from 44,000 to 108,000, and in Detroit it

Madam C. J. Walker

soared sevenfold from 5,700 to 40,800. African Americans were a growing element of urban America, and Indianapolis was not an exception to this rule.

Like the Slovenians and Bulgarians, the Black migrants generally had to settle for the dirtiest, most arduous jobs. Between 1916 and 1918, the number of African Americans working at the Kingan slaughterhouse doubled from 225 to 450. For generations Kingan seemed to serve as the first port of call for poor newcomers to the city. Irish, Slavic, and Black migrants all found jobs dispatching millions of hogs to their doom. Similarly, the number of Black employees at National Malleable rose 50 percent, from 300 to 450, between 1916 and 1918. Labor shortages resulting from workers enlisting in the armed forces and an increased demand for war matériel necessitated the hiring of Black laborers, many of whom had formerly been relegated to low-paying jobs as porters or servants. For migrants from the South, a position at Kingan or National Malleable seemed a step up from agricultural labor in Alabama or Mississippi.

On arriving in Indianapolis, the newcomers found a vibrant African American community. Indiana Avenue was the burgeoning center of Black life and offered African Americans a retailing alternative to white-dominated Washington Street. In 1916, in an eight-block area of the avenue, there were thirteen dry goods stores, sixteen tailors and clothing establishments, twenty-six grocers, thirty-three restaurants, and an equal number of saloons. The offices of lawyers, dentists, and physicians were evidence that some upwardly mobile Blacks were breaking into the professions. Perhaps the most notable symbol of African American success in Indianapolis was the Walker Manufacturing Company. Madam C. J. Walker had developed hair-care products for African Americans, and in 1916 her company grossed $119,000 in sales. She also invested in real estate, and after her death in 1919, her daughter fulfilled her dream of building a grand theater building on Indiana Avenue. It opened in 1927 and stood as a monument to Black enterprise. Another source of pride for the Black community was the Senate Avenue YMCA. Opened in

1913, it served as a center for African American life in Indianapolis, offering all the cultural, recreation, and religious programs available at its exclusively white counterparts.

The Indiana Avenue business district and Senate YMCA testified, however, to the city's persistent pattern of racial segregation. They existed because Blacks could not frequent white YMCAs or eat at white-owned restaurants in downtown Indianapolis. Indiana's capital was a racially bifurcated city with a Black heart along Indiana Avenue and a corresponding white center on Washington Street. It was a city sharply divided along racial lines.

This was evident in the city's elementary schools, which remained segregated, with Black teachers and pupils assigned to separate schools from their white counterparts. One purported advantage of this segregation was that it ensured more teaching positions for African Americans. In 1902, of the 585 teachers employed by the Indianapolis school board, fifty-three were Black. As yet the high schools remained exempt from this policy of mandatory segregation. Since the 1870s African Americans had attended the same high schools as whites, and this remained true on the eve of America's entry into World War I.

Southern Blacks migrating to Indianapolis did not escape racial segregation and did not leave behind interracial conflict. At times whites responded violently to any Black invasion of what they regarded as their turf. For example, in August 1901 more than 150 young whites attacked African Americans and chased them from Fairview Park. One Black man suffered a broken arm, and another was assailed with rocks and clubs. Such white gangs were known locally as bungaloos, and they seriously limited the freedom of African Americans. The crusading journalist Ray Stannard Baker investigated Black life in Indianapolis and in 1906 reported on the bungaloo gangs, "crowds of rough and lawless white boys who set upon Negroes and beat them frightfully, often wholly without provocation." These gangs were enforcers of a de facto form of segregation. Baker noted, "Although no law prevents Negroes from entering any park in Indianapolis, they are practically excluded from at least one of them by the danger of being assaulted by these gangs."[11] If the law did not create a racial barrier, the bungaloos compensated for this official negligence and used violence to keep African Americans in their supposed place.

Baker found that the attitudes of most Indianapolis whites toward Blacks ranged from indifference to hostility. He reported that "the only white people I could find who were much interested in Negroes were a few politicians, mostly of the lower sort, the charity workers and the police." He also quoted a local white man as saying, "There are too many Negroes up here; they hurt the city." Another responded to the increasing number of Blacks by concluding, "I suppose sooner or later we shall have to adopt some of the restrictions of the South."[12]

In 1910 journalist and local historian Jacob P. Dunn summarized what was probably the attitude of many white Indianapolis residents toward the Black migration. "Many objectionable negroes have come here, especially since the southern states began driving out their undesirable classes," Dunn observed. He further claimed, "It is generally understood that the disreputable class . . . are mostly recent importations, and not of the older negro families of the city."[13] During the first two decades of the twentieth century, bona fide Hoosier-born Blacks were not deemed such a problem. But the influx of newcomers from the South was viewed as cause for alarm.

Following World War I, Indianapolis whites responded to this alarm by taking action of the type commonplace in the Jim Crow South. During the 1920s the Ku Klux Klan won thousands of adherents in the Hoosier capital and, together with other like-minded groups, attempted to raise the barriers separating Blacks and whites. Indianapolis's white leadership unabashedly embraced racial segregation and endeavored to impose an even stricter code of racial separation than had previously existed.

In 1921 the Klan began to recruit members in Indianapolis. It was dedicated to white supremacy but also was anti-Catholic, anti-Jewish, and opposed to foreign immigration. The Klan presented itself as a defender of traditional white Protestant values. It was a foe of alcohol and a crusader against the sexual promiscuity that supposedly was corrupting America during the 1920s. Among the predominantly native-born white population of Indianapolis, Klan principles won support, and within a few years, an estimated 27 percent, and perhaps as high as 40 percent, of Indianapolis's native-born white males had joined the hooded fraternity.

Meanwhile, Indianapolis residents who were not necessarily associated with the Klan were lobbying for action that accorded with Klan principles. One demand was for the complete segregation of the schools. Though most of the elementary schools were already segregated, in a few cases, African American students could attend a white school if no Black school existed within a reasonable distance of the Black student's home. More significantly, the city's high schools had never segregated Blacks and whites. The majority of Indianapolis whites in the 1920s regarded such racial mixing as unacceptable. In 1922 the Federation of Civic Clubs petitioned the school board, arguing that the prevalence of tuberculosis among Blacks necessitated their separation from the white student population. A local organization calling itself the White Supremacy League joined the Mapleton Civic Association, a group largely dedicated to keeping Blacks out of the Mapleton neighborhood, in seconding the federation's call for separation of the races. That same year the Indianapolis Chamber of Commerce backed the proponents of segregation, calling on the school board to create a "separate, modern, completely equipped and adequate high school building for colored students."[14] Leading Blacks opposed these efforts. In a petition to the school board, the Better Indianapolis Civic League argued that it was "unjust, unAmerican, and against the spirit of democratic ideals that one section of the citizenship should subvert the funds of the common treasury to discriminate against another section solely on the basis of ancestry."[15]

Such arguments were to no avail, and in December 1922, the board adopted a report recommending a separate high school for African Americans. Moreover, in 1923 it adopted a policy of transferring the relatively few African Americans attending predominately white elementary schools to all-Black schools. In 1927 the all-Black Crispus Attucks High School received its first students, and until 1949 it was the city's only public secondary school open to African Americans. The Indianapolis schools were by law totally segregated according to race.

In the 1920s African Americans also endured segregation in the public parks. The city's superintendent of parks denied Blacks permission to hold events in parks that he designated as for white use only. African Americans were expected to restrict themselves to Douglass Park, which was created in 1921 to serve the Black community. Named for the famed Black abolitionist Frederick Douglass, the Jim Crow park was the recreational equivalent of Crispus Attucks High School. It was an African American reservation intended to thwart racial mixing in the increasingly divided Hoosier capital.

As the Black population rose, the threat of African Americans moving into white neighborhoods also increased. In response, white homeowners organized to halt the invasion of Blacks. For example, the Mapleton Civic Association unapologetically declared, "One of our chief concerns is to prevent members of the colored race from moving into our midst, thereby depreciating property values fifty per cent, or more."[16] Members of the Mapleton group pledged to sell or lease their properties solely to white persons.

Given such attitudes, Indianapolis was fertile ground in which to plant the Klan seed. The Klan flourished and soon demonstrated its political power. In the 1924 Republican primary, the Klan-backed candidate for governor defeated his anti-Klan opponent. Celebrating the victory, seven thousand Klansmen and Klanswomen marched in a victory parade from the north side through the Indiana Avenue neighborhood to the city center. In November the Republican Klan candidate, Edward Jackson, won the gubernatorial contest, and a Klan-endorsed slate carried the state offices, a majority of the state legislative seats, and the local seat in the United States House of Representatives. The following year a Klan candidate won the Indianapolis mayor's office, and the Klan also secured control of the city council. The association of the Klan with Republican candidates, however, cost the GOP the support of African American voters. For the first time since winning the right to vote in 1870, Indianapolis Blacks rejected the Republican ticket and voted Democrat.

In 1926 the Klan-endorsed city council fulfilled the dreams of groups such as the Mapleton Civic Association by adopting a residential segregation ordinance. Accepting a measure endorsed by the White Citizens Protective League, the council made it unlawful for whites to move into a "portion of the municipality inhabited principally by negroes," or for African Americans to take up residence in a white area, without receiving the written consent of a majority of the neighborhood's predominant race. Hundreds of cheering and clapping citizens jammed the council chamber to witness the passage of the measure, which the president of the White Citizens Protective League promised would "stabilize real estate values . . . and give the honest citizens and voters renewed faith in city officials."[17]

The cheering, however, was short lived. Eight months after its passage, the ordinance was held as unconstitutional in a case brought by the Indianapolis chapter of the National Association for the Advancement of Colored People (NAACP). The judge ruled that it violated the Fourteenth Amendment of the United States Constitution. Indianapolis could segregate its schools, but the city council could not use the law to segregate neighborhoods.

By the time of the decision, the Klan's political power was unraveling. Catholic, Jewish, and African American publications in Indianapolis had steadfastly attacked the Klan, opposing its bigotry and crusading for its defeat at the polls. Yet this opposition had failed to produce results. A scandal involving sex and murder proved more destructive than any high-minded editorial or well-argued essay on tolerance. The key figure in the scandal was David Curtis Stephenson, Indiana's grand dragon of the Ku Klux Klan. Stephenson was born in Texas and moved as a boy with his family to Oklahoma, where he became active in the Socialist Party. In 1920 he migrated north to Indiana, where he found his true calling as a recruiter for the Ku Klux Klan. Of the ten-dollar initiation fee he charged new Klan members, Stephenson kept four dollars for himself. He sold the robes and hoods worn by members for five to ten dollars and made a handsome profit from the sales. Within a short time, he was a wealthy man living in a mansion in the Irvington area of Indianapolis. As Indiana's grand dragon, he also exercised inordinate political influence. Political candidates seeking a Klan endorsement curried his favor.

In his personal life, however, Stephenson did not adhere to the Klan's devotion to sobriety and traditional moral values. Most notably, he did not uphold the chastity of white womanhood. On March 15, 1925, Stephenson and two of his henchmen abducted Madge Oberholtzer, a young statehouse secretary, and took her on a train headed for Chicago. According to Oberholtzer's testimony, Stephenson "took all my clothes off and pushed me into the lower berth," where he assaulted her brutally. Oberholtzer further claimed, "He chewed me all over my body, bit my neck and face, chewed my tongue, chewed my breasts until they bled, my back, my legs, my ankles, and mutilated me all over my body."[18] At Hammond, Indiana, the Stephenson party got off the train and checked into a hotel, where the distraught Oberholtzer took poison and began vomiting blood. Stephenson packed Oberholtzer in a car and drove her back to Indianapolis without obtaining any medical assistance for her. In Indianapolis the Stephenson party deposited Oberholtzer at her parents' house, where several physicians attended her. Oberholtzer made a dying declaration, describing the abduction and attack. On April 14, a month after the assault, Oberholtzer died.

Stephenson was arrested and, after a lengthy trial, was convicted of second-degree murder and sentenced to life imprisonment. The trial exposed all the sordid details of the crime and called into question the Klan's devotion to pure American values. Stephenson expected his political ally Governor Jackson to pardon him. When Jackson refused to do so, a bitter Stephenson retaliated by handing over evidence of the corrupt practices of Klan-endorsed public officials. The *Indianapolis Times* published a series of articles publicizing the corruption that earned it a Pulitzer Prize in 1928. The mayor of Indianapolis was forced to resign and served a short jail sentence. Six members of the city council also resigned in disgrace. Governor Jackson was indicted but escaped conviction because the statute of limitations precluded prosecution.

By the close of the 1920s, the disgraced Klan was virtually dead in Indianapolis and no longer had any political clout. The Klan was a short-lived phenomenon in the city's history. Yet the sentiments underlying the Klan and making it attractive to thousands of Indianapolis residents had a lasting impact on the city. Between 1917 and 1929, city leaders eschewed alien cultures and attempted to create a purely American city. The school board called for a city devoted to one nation, one language, and one flag and expunged German influence from the education system. The turnverein and Maennerchor survived, but German-language newspapers did not. Indianapolis was no longer a bilingual city with a proud Germanic element attempting to inculcate the glories of German culture into uncultivated Americans. Indianapolis was aiming to be a 100 percent American city.

Whereas the school board would not tolerate more than one national strain, it was dedicated to preserving and perpetuating an education system and city divided by race. There was a white city and a Black city, and white leaders seemed to believe that the two should remain separate and not trespass on each other's turf. In 1929 Indianapolis was more segregated racially than in 1917. It was a city proud of one united nationality but committed to maintaining the barriers between two races.

PROGRESS AND PROSPERITY

The first three decades of the twentieth century were an era of general prosperity and growth. There were momentary economic setbacks when business slowed and profits fell. In Indianapolis dozens of short-lived automakers closed their shops after

producing more debts than motor vehicles. No business investment was a sure thing. Yet the overall trajectory of the city was
upward as more Hoosiers found jobs and homes in the state's
capital. The city's population more than doubled, rising from
169,000 in 1900 to 364,000 in 1930. Indianapolis had reached
maturity, but it was not stagnant. It was sharing in the wave of
urbanization and economic growth sweeping the nation.

No institution was a better indicator of the nation's material
wealth than the downtown department store. The first half of
the twentieth century was the heyday of these giant emporiums.
Macy's and Gimbel's in New York City, Wanamaker's in Philadelphia, J. L. Hudson's in Detroit, and Marshall Field's in Chicago
were known throughout the nation. They were treasure troves
for eager shoppers and well-patronized symbols of America's
economic success. The retailing giants were storehouses of the
American dream.

Indianapolis was no exception to the triumph of the downtown department store. The big three retailers of the era in Indianapolis were L. S. Ayres, Block's, and H. P. Wasson. They offered a huge array of merchandise in ever-expanding stores that
enticed shoppers to spend as much as they possibly could. These
great emporiums sold goods but also sought to make shopping
a delightful experience for their largely female customers. Their
attractive window displays stirred the material fantasies of shoppers and lured them into the rich ambience of the handsomely
designed stores. The department store tearooms appealed to the
genteel aspirations of the ladies of Indiana, and a full range of
customer services were intended to make shopping a pleasure
rather than a chore. When female shoppers entered the retail
palaces, they were supposed to feel like special guests availing
themselves of the finest merchandise, at the most reasonable
prices, available in Indiana.

The largest of the big three was L. S. Ayres, a store that became the standard for female fashion in Indianapolis. In 1905
Ayres moved from the dry goods outlet it had occupied since
1875 to a grand new eight-story structure in the heart of the

L. S. Ayres department store

Washington Street shopping district. "On every hand were heard expressions of admiration for the magnificent interior," wrote a reporter describing the opening day. According to this observer, "From the dressmaking floor on the sixth floor to the economy store in the basement, the departments were in gala attire, and the choicest goods were on display. . . . The Paris gowns were rich beyond description. . . . A pink net with lace picked out in silver was the cynosure of feminine eyes." Another newspaper account wrote of 125 varieties of refreshment sold at the basement soda fountain, including "hot drinks, sour drinks, sundaes, mineral waters, fancy drinks, frappes, and more than a half dozen 'Ayres Specials' that tempt[ed] the thirsty."[19]

The new store was a great success, and the Ayres company built an addition doubling the size of the Washington Street building in 1915. Demanding ever more space, Ayres invested in another addition in 1929. This annex rose eleven stories and housed a new men's and boy's department. In 1922 Ayres celebrated its fiftieth anniversary and made a silent film publicizing the company's success. According to the film, the number of Ayres employees rose from 238 in 1905, prior to the opening of the new store, to 1,100 in 1922. In 1922 the store had 6.17 acres of floor space and employed buying officers in such major centers as New York, London, Paris, and Berlin but also in the more exotic Asian ports of Yokohama and Manila. The message was clear. Ayres was a huge emporium offering goods from throughout the world for Indiana shoppers. In further recognition of its golden anniversary, Ayres held a two-week storewide sale that it publicized over the two-week period with multipage advertisements in the city's daily newspapers. On the opening day of the sale, thirty-one thousand shoppers, equal to one-tenth of the city's population, filled the store aisles.

Rivaling Ayres was the William H. Block Company. In 1911 more than seventy thousand people attended the opening of Block's newly erected eight-story outlet. In a formal announcement, the store's management dedicated "this magnificent new store" to "the People of the State of Indiana, and Especially to the Home Folks of Indianapolis," and proclaimed it "the Pride of Hoosierdom."[20] Located across the street from the Traction Terminal, Block's would become the first stop for thousands of shoppers arriving on interurbans from the small towns and rural areas of Indiana. As such it had an advantage over Ayres one block farther south on Washington Street, as an interurban shopper who found everything she wanted at Block's had no need to walk the extra distance to Ayres.

H. P. Wasson and Company also attracted a loyal clientele. According to a publication boosting the city of Indianapolis and extolling its retail advantages, in 1907 Wasson's already consisted of "sixty-six departments, each a complete store within itself," and employed more than six hundred persons. Each of Wasson's dressmaking departments was headed by "an expert modiste" who visited "Europe twice a year, thus keeping in touch with the creations of the most notable European artist-modistes."[21]

Located across Washington Street from Ayres, Wasson's was a convenient alternative to its larger neighbor. If a shopper could not find what she wanted at Ayres, she could cross the street and try Wasson's. If the sought-after item was not at either Ayres or Wasson's, it probably did not exist.

Ayres, Block's, and Wasson's were only part of the retail picture in Indianapolis. According to the nation's first retail census, in 1929 there were 4,920 stores in the city employing more than twenty-three thousand full-time workers. The 1,757 food stores accounted for 21 percent of all sales, and the 59 motor vehicle showrooms contributed nearly 12 percent of local retail revenues. There were 392 gasoline stations serving the newly purchased automobiles and 584 restaurants satisfying local appetites. Enjoying the last year of prosperity before the Great Depression, Indianapolis consumers were emptying their wallets and filling the tills of retailers.

Another sign of urban success in the early twentieth century was the widespread construction of skyscraper office buildings. With steel-frame construction, buildings could rise to unprecedented heights, transforming the skylines of cities throughout the United States. Three- or four-story Victorian relics yielded to high-rise symbols of modernity and prosperity. A city's success was to a large degree measured by the height of its buildings. Climaxing the race to the skies was the construction of New York City's Empire State Building, which on completion in 1931 soared 102 stories and 1,250 feet.

In Indianapolis many older buildings gave way to new steel-framed structures. The Odd Fellows Building completed in 1908 rose sixteen stories, and the Fletcher Trust Building, which opened in 1915, likewise offered sixteen stories of office space. The city's tallest office building was the Merchants National Bank Building completed in 1913. It was 245 feet high with seventeen stories and remained the city's tallest office structure until 1962. Other office buildings followed in the 1920s, such as the 200-foot, fifteen-story National City Bank Building; the 160-foot, twelve-floor Roosevelt Building; and the 152-foot, ten-story Illinois Building.

As in other cities, these new structures rose far above the commercial buildings remaining from the 1870s and 1880s, yet what actually distinguished Indianapolis was the absence of skyscrapers equal to those in many cities of comparable population. By the early 1930s, Cincinnati's Carew Tower soared forty-eight stories (574 feet), the American Insurance Union Citadel in Columbus rose forty-seven stories (555 feet), the First National Bank in Saint Paul had thirty-two stories (417 feet), and the Foshay Tower in Minneapolis was Minnesota's tallest building at thirty-two stories and 447 feet. From 1930 to 1962, the tallest building in Indiana was not in the state's largest city but in much smaller Fort Wayne, where the 312-foot, twenty-two-story Lincoln Bank Building claimed the distinction.

Instead of becoming a high-rise metropolis, Indianapolis sprouted a number of mid-rise buildings, basically two-hundred-foot shafts topped by flat roofs, rather than tapering towers or soaring spires. The city's office building developers did not share the hubris of Block's or Ayres and did not seek to create skyscrapers that would be the pride of Hoosierdom. They deferred to Fort Wayne, leaving the city's skyline of 1960 pretty much what it had been during the second decade of the century. Whereas the Merchants National Bank was the tallest building in the city, the tallest structure was the 284-foot Soldiers and Sailors Monument. For six decades this icon of the city dominated the skyline, demonstrating that Indianapolis was a city of commemoration as well as commerce.

Among the new buildings erected in the city between 1900 and 1930 were a number of hotels that offered visitors lodging equal to that available in the largest American cities. Perhaps the city's premier hotel was the Claypool. When it opened in 1903, it boasted of having the largest lobby in the United States. Moreover, all its rooms had private baths, a rare amenity in an age when most hotel guests had to go down the hall to use a shared

Claypool Hotel

bathroom. During the second decade of the century, the city witnessed the construction of other new hostelries that competed for the trade of travelers and the growing number of convention goers. In 1912 the seventeen-story Washington Hotel opened, offering three hundred rooms with baths. The following year the Severin Hotel welcomed its first guests. Its proximity to Union Station was a decided advantage since virtually all overnight lodgers in the early twentieth century arrived by train. With a decor reminiscent of the reign of France's Sun King, the hotel's Louis XIV Café offered fine dining to its hungry patrons. In 1918 the Hotel Lincoln joined the list of new hotels. Its grand dining room was sheathed in travertine marble, and a custom-made organ entertained patrons at the Sunday evening dinner concerts.

Perhaps the grandest hotel of the era was located not downtown but on the north side. Realizing the dream of successful shoe retailer George Marott, the Marott Hotel opened at its north-side location in 1926 and became the favorite of many of the city's most distinguished visitors. Much admired for its open-air Spanish garden, the Marott featured the marble pillars and crystal chandeliers that had become necessary ornaments of all fine hotels in the early twentieth century. The Marott, like its downtown competitors, sent visitors the message that Indianapolis was a big city with which to be reckoned. It was the crossroads of America capable of accommodating thousands of guests in a manner worthy of New York City or Chicago.

Among the other new structures arising in Indianapolis were a growing number of downtown movie theaters. Moviegoing was becoming the passion of the age, and in Indianapolis, as elsewhere, entertainment-hungry city dwellers flocked to first-run theaters downtown to see their favorite stars in the latest offerings from Hollywood. In 1912 the new 1,400 seat Lyric Theater opened, and over the following half century, it offered vaudeville acts and live musical performances as well as motion pictures. In the 1920s the Lyric management redecorated the theater's interior in an effort to match the grandeur of rival entertainment palaces. French mirrors, crystal chandeliers, and marble wainscoting adorned its elaborate gold and ivory lobby. The Lyric also acquired what purported to be the largest theater organ in Indiana. In 1916 the 3,100-seat Circle Theatre opened on Monument Circle, becoming one of the city's premier cinema venues. The Loew's Theatre welcomed its first customers in 1921. With 2,548 seats, it, like the Circle Theatre, was a downtown mecca for moviegoers. Adding to the options for Indianapolis audiences was the Apollo Theatre, which began screening films in 1922.

The most elaborate downtown movie palace, however, was the Indiana Theatre on Washington Street. Its glazed white terra cotta facade was in the Spanish baroque style, and its lobby featured travertine marble and ornate plaster decoration. With 3,200 seats, it was Indianapolis's largest movie palace. But its greatest distinction was the Indiana Roof Ballroom, which occupied the top floor of the theater building. Designed to resemble a Spanish town square, the ballroom featured a domed blue ceiling complete with small electric stars. The theater's facade, lobby, auditorium, and ballroom together presented a fantasy of old Spain. For the modest price of admission, Indianapolis movie-goers could watch their celluloid favorites in an ambience far removed from everyday Hoosier life. Given its name, it is ironic that the Indiana Theatre was a place designed to make patrons forget they were in Indiana.

The ballroom of the Indiana Theatre, the tearoom and Paris-inspired fashions at Ayres, the Louis XIV Café of the Severin, and the Spanish garden at the Marott were all alternatives to the sometimes-harsh realities of Indianapolis existence. They were carefully manufactured spaces far removed from the hog butchering of the Kingan plant, the shanties of Slavic immigrants and Black newcomers, the racial tensions of a Klan-dominated city, and the sexual bestiality of men like D. C. Stephenson. They constituted the other side of Indianapolis, a city where a housewife could be treated like a high-class lady at Ayres, a convention-going Knight of Pythias could sup in an environment inspired by a French king, and shoe clerks could dance under artificial stars in an ersatz Spanish plaza. The owners of department stores, hotels, and movie palaces knew that a touch of class and a serving of glamour would make money, and they responded accordingly.

The most monumental showplace of the city, however, was not a department store, hotel, or theater but instead a redevelopment project commemorating those who fought in World War I. In 1919 the city of Indianapolis successfully campaigned to secure the national headquarters of the American Legion, a veterans' organization founded in the aftermath of the war. As part of the deal with the legion, the city and the state of Indiana promised to build a memorial honoring World War I veterans. In 1920 the Indiana legislature appropriated $2 million for this memorial, which would span five blocks north of Monument Circle. Two small public parks already occupied part of the site, but other spaces had to be cleared of existing buildings, one of which was the Indiana School for the Blind dating from the mid-nineteenth century. Plans for the monumental plaza and memorial building accorded with City Beautiful tenets of planning, which had influenced American urban development since the 1890s. City Beautiful planners sought to re-create American cities with neoclassical civic centers replete with statuary and fountains. According to the City Beautiful ideal, the American city should be transformed into an uplifting place of beauty that would inspire residents to higher ideals than simply the making of money. For City Beautiful planners, the city was to be a place of civic celebration as well as a commercial hub.

In 1923 the War Memorial Board selected a Cleveland architectural firm to design the project, which would include a headquarters building for the legion, a cenotaph, an obelisk, and, most important, a grand neoclassical memorial structure as the monumental centerpiece. The architects patterned the memorial building after the Mausoleum of Halicarnassus, one of the ancient seven wonders of the world, though the Indianapolis version was to be seventy-five feet taller and thus even grander than the ancient original. On July 4, 1927, General John Pershing laid the cornerstone for the structure, but construction proceeded slowly. The interior was not dedicated until November 11, 1933, though some of it was still unfinished. Meanwhile, work was completed on the one-hundred-foot black granite obelisk and surrounding fountain and the cenotaph, which memorialized Corporal James Gresham of Evansville, Indiana, the first American soldier killed in action in World War I.

The memorial building was a magnificent structure sheathed in Indiana limestone and approached by grand stairways on its north and south sides. On the south side was Pro Patria, a colossal male nude twenty-five feet high. When created in 1929, it was purported to be the largest bronze sculpture ever cast in the United States. Atop six huge columns on the building's exterior were additional figures sculpted in stone representing Courage, Memory, Peace, Victory, Liberty, and Patriotism. The highlight of the interior was the Shrine Room, a space soaring 115 feet in height with a giant American flag and a crystal "Star of Destiny" hanging from the vaulted ceiling. Marble wainscoting and columns added to the grandeur, as did a molded frieze depicting the Allied struggle for peace. At the center of the room, beneath the flag, was an altar constructed of a rich variety of marbles.

Overall, the War Memorial Plaza was a worthy complement to the iconic Soldiers and Sailors Monument. Both expressed Hoosier patriotism with an exuberance not matched elsewhere in the nation. Indianapolis could not claim the tallest buildings among cities of its size, but it was unsurpassed as a city of commemoration. The War Memorial Plaza was one of the finest examples of City Beautiful planning in the nation and proof that the Hoosier capital did not exist simply to slaughter hogs and race cars. Indianapolis was a city of soaring monuments and grand commemorative spaces and was not reluctant to declare its devotion to the nation and to those who sacrificed their lives in the nation's wars.

During the first decades of the twentieth century, another ensemble of buildings testified to Indianapolis's emergence as a major medical center. In 1908 three private medical schools merged to form Indiana University School of Medicine, based in Indianapolis. In 1914 the Robert W. Long Hospital opened on the near west side as a training facility for the school's students, and five years later, the medical school moved its classrooms and offices from downtown to Emerson Hall, adjacent to Long Hospital. Riley Hospital for Children began serving the public on the medical campus in 1924, earning a distinguished reputation for pediatric care. The William Coleman Hospital for Women joined the other buildings at the site when it opened in 1927, and the Ball Residence for Nurses was dedicated the following year. By 1929, then, Indianapolis had become a notable center for medical care and education. Even more important, these early twentieth-century facilities laid the foundation for a medical center that would burgeon into a major element in the city's future economy. In 1929 Indianapolis's prosperity still rested on a base of rail transportation, manufacturing, and commerce in general. Ninety years later, the medical center would be an all-important foundation stone of a far-different local economy.

Complementing the services of the medical center were the contributions of Eli Lilly and Company to the health of millions of people throughout the world. The Lilly company had become a prominent local industry during the late nineteenth century, but in the 1920s, it reached new heights and established a world-wide reputation as a center of pharmaceutical research and production. In 1919 the British scientist George Clowes was hired as Lilly's director of biochemical research, and in this role, he introduced a new level of expertise in the company and, most notably, developed the commercial production of insulin. Clowes had become aware of the work of scientists at the University of Toronto who had developed a pancreatic extract they called insulin. When injected in diabetic patients, the extract reduced blood sugar to acceptable levels and enabled diabetics to resume normal lives. The Canadian scientists were stymied, however, in their efforts to produce the life-saving drug in large batches. In 1922 Clowes and Eli Lilly, the company founder's grandson, negotiated a deal with the Toronto researchers. The Lilly company would solve the production problem and make insulin available to diabetes patients throughout the world.

By 1923 the Indianapolis concern was able to market insulin, and Lilly not only saved lives but profited handsomely. In its first year on the market, sales of the Lilly brand of insulin reached $1.1 million, triple the amount earned by any previous product in a single year. Insulin made Eli Lilly and Company a prime contender among American pharmaceutical concerns and Indianapolis a name to be reckoned with as a drug manufacturing center. Recognizing the importance of insulin for the maturing of the company, one employee observed, "We got our first pair of long pants in 1922." In later years J. K. Lilly Sr., the head of the Lilly clan, judged the significance of insulin. "When one contemplates the history of this item and what it has meant to this company," he wrote, "it makes the heart glow with pride and thankfulness. . . . Insulin revolutionized our place in the industry and put us on the way to present and future greatness."[22]

During the first three decades of the twentieth century, Indianapolis lost the contest for automotive supremacy to Detroit but emerged as a major player in the field of pharmaceuticals. Moreover, the Indiana University Medical Center was laying the foundation for its later importance as a leading employer in the city. The dense interurban network was boosting sales at downtown department stores, and as a major crossroads for steam railroads in the nation, Indianapolis was attracting convention goers and commercial travelers to hotels that ranked with the best in the nation. Its movie palaces ensured that Indianapolis audiences could enjoy the best Hollywood fare. At the close of the 1920s, Indianapolis was in many ways a mature, successful city, and it also seemed to have a bright future.

DEPRESSION AND WAR

In September 1929 Ayres opened its eleven-story annex amid expectations of ever-rising sales and profits. The store's management looked forward to another decade of prosperity that would warrant the creation of ever-increasing sales space. The following month the stock market crashed, blighting dreams of a bright future and ushering in ten grim years of economic distress. In Indianapolis and throughout the nation, economic indicators plummeted and then rebounded to a degree but were never cause for celebration. World War II boosted the economy but resulted in four years of severe restrictions on construction and consumption as Indianapolis and the nation focused on defeating the Axis powers. By the fall of 1945, Indianapolis had experienced sixteen years during which many civic improvements had been on hold, and the city had been forced to delay initiatives aimed at upgrading its infrastructure and built environment.

During the first year following the stock market crash, Indianapolis felt the consequences of the deteriorating economy. By September 1930 the number of persons employed in Indianapolis had fallen 17 percent below the figure for 1929. The economy continued to worsen, and in November 1931, the employment figure was 25 percent below the pre-Depression level. Five months later the drop from 1929 had widened to 30 percent. The impact on manufacturing jobs was especially severe. The manufacturing workforce dropped from 59,714 in 1930 to approximately 30,000 in 1933.

As funds available for investment and consumption shrank, construction was at a virtual standstill. In 1933 the building index in the city was down nearly 90 percent from the late 1920s level. That year only twenty-seven houses were built in the entire city of Indianapolis. Carpenters, bricklayers, and masons were idle, joining thousands of out-or-work factory hands in the growing army of the unemployed.

Plummeting sales forced many vulnerable businesses to close. During the Depression years, the city's three remaining automakers all ceased production. Marmon, Stutz, and Duesenberg produced luxury cars on a relatively small scale for the affluent. Unlike Ford or General Motors, they did not serve the mass market but depended on customers who could afford the finest automobiles. As the Depression deepened, the number of buyers who could pay for luxury declined, shrinking the number of consumers in the market for the fine automobiles of Indianapolis. Forced to face reality, Marmon ceased auto production in 1933, Stutz did so in 1935, and Duesenberg was dissolved in 1937. Indianapolis had ceded any claim to the title Motor City to Detroit at least two decades earlier, but a few local automakers had lingered on. By the close of the Depression decade, however, the city was no longer the headquarters of any auto manufacturer. It continued to make auto parts and serve the auto industry in a subsidiary role, yet the fine motorcars that had been the pride of Indianapolis were consigned to the pages of automotive histories.

The interurbans suffered the same fate. During the 1920s the electric railroads had continued to carry thousands of passengers despite increasing competition from automobiles, but they could not survive the Depression. Throughout the 1930s the interurban companies abandoned lines, and the number of cars arriving in and departing from Indianapolis daily dropped from 387 in 1929 to 125 in 1938. As electric rail traffic slackened, the Traction Terminal management paved over tracks at the depot, transforming it into a bus station. Finally, in 1941, the last interurban car made the run into Indianapolis. The age of the electric railroad was over.

There was some improvement in business after 1933 as President Franklin Roosevelt's New Deal pumped federal money into the economy. Thousands of unemployed workers in Indianapolis received relief money. In March 1935 nearly 19 percent of Marion County residents were relief recipients. The federal Public Works Administration (PWA) invested in building projects, which provided jobs for construction workers. One of these PWA initiatives was Lockefield Gardens, a large-scale, low-rent housing project in the heart of the city's principal African American neighborhood. Twenty-two acres of slum housing were cleared to make way for the project, which won accolades when completed in 1938. It was composed of 748 dwelling units in twenty-four brick buildings of two to four stories. Tenants enjoyed ample open space, as a handsome grassy mall extended through the center of the project. Lockefield Gardens also included playgrounds and a small shopping area for the convenience of residents. Providing modern, sanitary housing in place of virtually uninhabitable shanties, Lockefield Gardens was acclaimed as a model housing development. If cities throughout the nation followed the example of this Indianapolis project, it seemed to promise a slum-free future for urban America. Reflecting the prevailing racial attitudes of the period, Lockefield Gardens was segregated. It housed only African Americans and thus perpetuated residential racial segregation in Indianapolis. Yet for the project's initial Black residents, it offered a marked improvement in their living standards. Moreover, the $3 million expended on the construction of Lockefield Gardens put money in the pockets of grateful local construction workers.

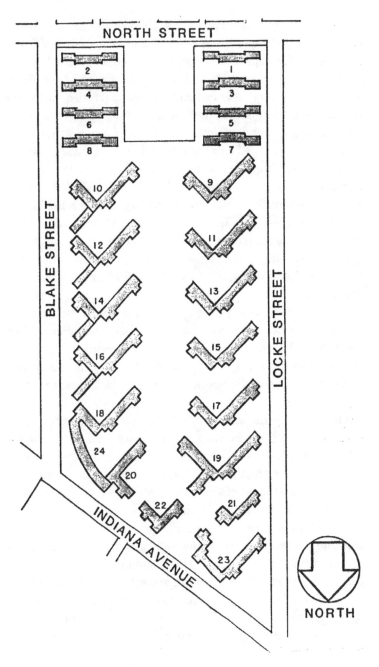

A plan of Lockefield Gardens

By the mid-1930s there was also some revival of private investment, which generated jobs for distressed Indianapolis residents. In 1934 Block's department store launched an expansion and modernization project, nearly doubling the size of its establishment and installing new furnishings and amenities, including stainless steel escalators. Then, in 1937, Wasson's Washington Street emporium underwent a radical transformation. On completion, the renovated store was model of style moderne architecture, clad in limestone and granite with vertical glass strips in place of traditional windows. The store installed the latest form of illumination, fluorescent lighting, thus precluding the need for natural light. The renovated Wasson's store was a sleek, up-to-date structure standing out from many of its dowdy Washington Street neighbors. It also testified to the continued willingness of the city's major retailers to invest in a still-distressed Indianapolis.

Another encouraging development was the construction of a major new International Harvester plant on Indianapolis's southeast side. It opened in 1938, producing motors for International Harvester trucks. It also provided 1,100 much-needed jobs and raised hopes for economic recovery in the still-beleaguered capital city.

One existing Indianapolis industry struck a positive note throughout much of the 1930s and mitigated some of the worst effects of the Depression. Eli Lilly and Company adopted a policy of not laying off any employees. Throughout the 1930s, Lilly workers were ensured of a paycheck. Moreover, during the very depths of the Depression in the summer of 1933, Lilly began construction on a new research laboratory that was completed the following year. The company could afford such largess, as its sales remained strong despite the economic downturn. For the years 1920–1929, total sales were $89,977,000; for the Depression decade of 1930–1939, the figure was $171,684,000. Basically, for Lilly, one of Indianapolis's largest businesses, there was no Depression. Further benefiting the city was the creation of the

Lilly Endowment in 1937. During its early years, the endowment's philanthropy was relatively modest. But it would grow to became a major benefactor for the city and state, sharing the company's good fortune with the Hoosier public.

Though there was some good news, the overall picture for the decade was bleak. As late as 1940, there were 10 percent fewer people employed in Indianapolis than in 1930. The drop in employment among African Americans was especially severe, as the number of Blacks with a job fell 27 percent over the decade. Population figures also reflected the impact of the Depression. Indianapolis's population increased only 6 percent between 1930 and 1940, the slowest pace for any ten-year period since the city's founding. This conformed to the national pattern; the number of inhabitants in the nation as a whole rose at a lower rate than in any previous decade. Indianapolis performed better than northern industrial cities such as Cleveland, Saint Louis, and Philadelphia, which lost population for the first time in their histories. Yet the 1940 data likely brought little solace to Indianapolis boosters. The city was not as bad off as some places, but it was surviving rather than thriving.

The United States' entry into World War II radically changed the economic picture. Local plants expanded their facilities and hired thousands of additional employees to meet the demand for materials necessary for the war effort. The most notable local defense contractor was the Allison Division of General Motors. Founded as a machine shop by James Allison—Carl Fisher's partner in Prest-O-Lite and the Indianapolis Speedway—the Allison works were purchased by General Motors following its founder's death. During the 1930s, it developed a superior aircraft engine, and it produced seventy thousand engines for the Allied war effort in World War II. At its peak of production in 1943, Allison employed twenty-three thousand workers. Among its achievements was the production of the nation's first jet engine.

Other Indianapolis manufacturers also made notable contributions to the Allied victory in World War II. The Naval Ordnance

Plant manufactured the Norden bombsight, which enabled high-altitude American bombers to hit enemy targets. Indianapolis's Curtiss-Wright factory turned out propellers for Allied aircraft, and the International Harvester facility produced engines used in military vehicles as well as navy antiaircraft gun mounts. Eli Lilly and Company worked to develop penicillin, which could save the lives of injured service personnel. Employment figures reflected the high demand for goods related to the war. By the summer of 1944, an estimated 135,000 workers were employed in Indianapolis industries, more than double the number in 1930.

Local military installations further boosted the economy and served the war effort. Fort Benjamin Harrison in northeast Marion County, established in 1904, had played a vital role in training and mobilizing troops during World War I. Following a period of quiescence during the 1920s and 1930s, the post again became a hub of activity during World War II. In the early 1940s, it was the nation's largest induction center, processing the new recruits and draftees who would defeat the Axis powers. In addition to its role as an induction center, the fort served a multitude of military functions. At Fort Benjamin Harrison, the two-thousand-bed Billings General Hospital treated casualties of war, a school produced cooks and bakers for the armed forces, an army finance center trained financial specialists, an army disciplinary facility housed 2,700 prisoners, and an additional 550 German and Italian prisoners of war were held at the fort.

Meanwhile, on the southwest side of the city, Stout Field became a base for the Army Air Corps. Originally intended to serve as Indianapolis's municipal airfield, it proved too small for that purpose and in 1931 was superseded by what would become Indianapolis International Airport. During World War II, the underused field became home to a troop carrier command that directed air transport operations. The Indianapolis Naval Armory, completed in 1938 on the north side of the city, trained radio operators for the navy. Though landlocked and far from any navigable body of water, Indianapolis did its part to ensure American victory at sea.

Because of the city's central location at the intersection of some of the nation's busiest railroads, millions of military personnel passed through Indianapolis and crowded the waiting room at Union Station. Centers opened to welcome, feed, and entertain the many transients and personnel stationed in the city. The Union Station Canteen was open twenty-four hours a day; over the course of the war, it supplied meals to two million service personnel. Churches also hosted military transients, and a club in the city's African American district offered food and refuge for Black soldiers. By 1943 there were fourteen service centers in Indianapolis to boost the spirits and aid the morale of the armed forces that passed through the crossroads of America.

The war forced marked changes in the lives of Indianapolis civilians. With thousands of newcomers arriving in the city to take jobs in the booming defense plants, housing became a premium commodity. Wartime restrictions seriously limited residential construction, forcing the many migrants from rural areas and small towns to crowd into existing and often substandard housing. Rationing meant that Indianapolis residents had to cut back on their purchases and forgo certain activities. In 1942 L. S. Ayres canceled its annual anniversary sale, explaining that the traditional shopping extravaganza did "not fit in a world of restrictions, shortages, patriotism and rationing." It was "as out of place as two-thousand-mile auto trips and four lumps of sugar in your third cup of coffee."[23] Rationing of gasoline and tires, as well as a halt to automobile production during the war years, had an especially marked impact on travel patterns within the city. Indianapolis residents crowded public transit as ridership on streetcars and buses surged. There was momentary relief from automobile congestion on the city streets. Memorial Day weekends also became less harried as the Indianapolis Speedway suspended the running of the Indianapolis 500 race for the duration of the war. From 1942 through 1945, Indianapolis did not host its signature event.

Restrictions on construction and labor shortages owing to the thousands of local men and women needed for the armed forces and defense work meant that the city government also suspended major projects. The city could maintain existing basic services but little else. In Indianapolis and other major cities, however, local leaders were looking to the future and considering what needed to be done once the war was over. Thus, committees organized in cities across the nation to provide blueprints for postwar development. In 1943 Indianapolis mayor Robert Tyndall appointed a committee of 150 leading citizens to draft such a plan for the Hoosier capital.

In October 1944 this Committee on Postwar Planning presented its findings at a dinner held in Block's department store. In his opening remarks, the meeting's host, store executive Meier S. Block, set the tone of the report when he announced, "It is time for us business and professional men of Indianapolis to raise our sights and to think about the future of our home town in a more heroic manner." The committee emphasized the need to improve the city's sewer system and combat the smoke pollution generated by the burning of bituminous coal. Underlying the recommendations, however, was concern about physical blight in the center of the city and decentralization of the population to the outskirts and even beyond the city limits. The civic leaders feared that Indianapolis was rotting at its core and that the rot was encouraging the outward movement of population that was detrimental to the city's future. According to the committee chair, all the committee's "thinking, and all its plans . . . [were] geared to the goal of reversing this trend toward decentralization."[24]

Indianapolis leaders needed to make the city a desirable place to live, with upgraded thoroughfares to accommodate the increased automobile traffic of the postwar world and with an aggressive program of slum clearance to stem the growth of blight, which would drive people from the city. The committee chair noted that some other older cities had become ringed by a "Chinese wall" of suburban municipalities that "prevent[ed] normal growth and deaden[ed] the central city." He was grateful that Indianapolis had as yet avoided that fate but believed action was necessary to forestall any acceleration of the decentralization that was so damaging to the city. The committee was, however, determined that all its plans should be realized without aid from the federal government. The chair most definitively asserted, "We don't want any recurrence of federal aid." Indianapolis should finance its own improvement "without going begging to Washington for any further extension of the evils of federal aid and federal domination over local units of government."[25]

By the close of the war, Indianapolis leaders were facing the fact that Indianapolis was a mature city confronting the problems of an aging core. Neighborhoods were deteriorating, and the threat of spreading blight seemed real. Parts of the city needed reconstructive surgery if Indianapolis was to continue to attract residents and ward off the challenge from new construction in outlying areas. Yet it was also an independent city. After a dozen years of massive federal spending aimed at combating economic depression and the military threat of the Axis powers, Indianapolis leaders were eschewing any further interference from Washington. Indianapolis realized the need for change and aggressive local government action. But they embraced a conservative aversion to an interfering Washington bureaucracy and sought to remake their mature city on their own.

4

Expansion and Renewal
1945 –2000

In 1944 the Committee on Postwar Planning identified decentralization of the metropolitan population and blight of central areas as key problems facing Indianapolis. Throughout the second half of the twentieth century, policymakers remained focused on these two factors that seemed so threatening to the city's viability. Facilitated by the widespread ownership of automobiles, residents and businesses moved outward at an unprecedented pace, diminishing the significance of the urban core. During the middle of the century, once-fine neighborhoods deteriorated, and worried civic leaders witnessed the decline and decay of formerly prime properties in the downtown Mile Square. Concern about the city's spreading blight and poor image elicited aggressive revitalization later in the century and a concerted effort to restore and renovate older areas of the city. Reflecting the postwar committee's reluctance to accept federal aid, Indianapolis rejected federal urban renewal funding in the 1950s, but federal financing of interstate highways transformed the city's landscape, as did federal programs to encourage homeownership. Moreover, in the latter part of the century, interference by a federal judge seeking racial equity disrupted the status quo in public education. Indianapolis could not escape the reach of the federal government as it coped with decentralization and racial change.

DECENTRALIZATION AND DECLINE

Each succeeding federal census recorded the outward movement of the city's population and the decentralization of the metropolis. Between 1950 and 1980, the population of Center Township, which encompassed the historic core of the city, fell 38 percent. During that period this central area lost 128,000 people; in 1980 it was home to 10,000 fewer residents than in 1910. In contrast, the combined population of Marion County's eight outlying townships soared 161 percent. In 1950 Center Township held 61 percent of the county's population; in 1980 this figure had fallen to 26 percent. Over three decades the Indianapolis area went from a city with its population concentrated in the core to a metropolis sprawling throughout the county's four hundred square miles.

The change was especially notable in the 1950s, when the combined population of the outer townships increased a remarkable 75 percent. Some townships were transformed over a few short years. The population of Lawrence Township, in the northwestern corner of Marion County, rose fourfold during the 1950s from 8,577 to 34,405. Housing developments sprouted in former cornfields, and in the Lawrence area and elsewhere along the Indianapolis fringe, rural backwaters quick-changed into suburban expanses of ranch homes and auto-clogged highways. A person who left Lawrence Township in 1950 would not have recognized the area upon returning in 1960. The expanding metropolis had engulfed it and made it a far different place.

Indianapolis's sprawling development was typical of metropolitan growth in the United States during the mid-twentieth century. Throughout the nation, the postwar demand for new housing in the late 1940s and the 1950s fueled a boom in residential construction. World War II and Korean War veterans sought to realize the American dream they had defended by purchasing houses with all the modern amenities, including a yard with space for their growing number of children. One Indianapolis builder who sought to meet this demand was Gene Glick. After returning from service in World War II, he and his wife, Marilyn, began building houses on a small scale, completing four houses in 1947–1948 and doubling that number the following year. Soon they expanded their operations, focusing on the construction of moderate-priced homes on the city's far east side. Western Electric, Ford, Chrysler, and RCA had built major plants along Shadeland Avenue on the east side, employing thousands of workers who were potential homeowners. To serve these customers, the Glicks opted to build prefabricated houses manufactured by the National Homes Company of Lafayette, Indiana. In 1956 they launched the Sycamore Heights development of 148 National Homes dwellings. Encouraged by the success of this project, they embarked on the construction of 219 houses in East Sycamore Heights in early 1957. By the close of the 1950s, the Glick company accounted for 12 percent of the building market in Marion County. It was constructing about two houses a day and as many as 500 each year. It surpassed this in the early 1960s, building 1,111 houses from 1961 to 1962, primarily on Indianapolis's burgeoning far east side.

The Glicks were not the only Indianapolis builders erecting affordable prefabricated housing for working-class and lower-middle-class buyers. On the northwest side, the giant Eagledale subdivision was also ensuring that National Homes left its imprint on Indianapolis. As in the Glick developments, low-interest, long-term mortgages insured by the Federal Housing Administration and the Veterans Administration made the new homes affordable to many less affluent Indianapolis residents. Federal policy encouraged homeownership and fueled the decentralization of Indianapolis. Advertisements for Eagledale from the mid-1950s promised three-bedroom homes priced from $9,975, or $67 per month with no down payment for qualified veterans. This was a deal few prospective buyers could pass up. By 1960, only six years after the opening of the development, Eagledale was home to 12,258 residents living in 3,025 houses. The houses were small, with National Homes having masterfully crammed three bedrooms and one bath into the modest structures. But courtesy of the federal government's mortgage insurance programs, Eagledale did provide homeownership and suburban living for a class of people who could not have afforded it in earlier decades.

Postwar builders, however, were not only accommodating the working and lower middle classes. They were also custom building thousands of new homes for the affluent. In northern Marion County, the population of the well-heeled community of Meridian Hills increased 155 percent during the 1950s as expensive new homes filled vacant lots. Nearby, the population of exclusive Williams Creek rose fourfold between 1940 and 1960. The upper-middle-class, far-north-side neighborhood of Arden had been platted in 1927, but the Depression of the 1930s put home construction on hold. During the late 1940s and early 1950s, Arden, like neighboring Meridian Hills, filled up with new houses for Indianapolis residents seeking homes farther from the city center. The small-scale construction in affluent north Marion County did not attract as much attention as the mass erection of National Homes dwellings on the far east side or in Eagledale. But it was part of the same phenomenon. Both the working class and the city's elite were moving outward, expanding the footprint of metropolitan development to the county's fringes.

As consumers moved outward, so did retailers. Throughout the nation, the 1950s and 1960s witnessed the rapid development of suburban shopping centers. They provided a full range of merchandise formerly only found downtown at locations conveniently close to shoppers' homes. Moreover, they offered ample parking, a major advantage in the automobile age. By 1960, 81 percent of Marion County households owned automobiles, and twenty years later, this figure had risen to 88 percent. In 1980, 49 percent of the county's households owned two or more cars. Automobiles were ubiquitous; everyone who could do so was driving, and they wanted a place to park. Outlying shopping centers surrounded by a vast expanse of paved parking space thus fit shoppers' needs. They offered a broad inventory of goods and spared consumers the long trek to downtown stores. And one could always find a convenient parking space at the suburban centers.

Eastgate Shopping Center, on the fast-growing east side, was the first of its kind in the Indianapolis area. Opening in 1957, it included outlets of J. C. Penney company and Sears and, perhaps most important, the first outlying branch of the H. P. Wasson department store. For shoppers seeking bargain merchandise not sold by the esteemed department store, the center also housed the five-and-dime retailers G. C. Murphy and Woolworth's.

Even more impressive was the Glendale Shopping Center, which opened on the north side in 1958. Branches of Block's and Ayres stood at opposite ends of the center's open-air concourse. At Glendale a total of forty-five stores served the more affluent clientele of Indianapolis's north side. It was a showplace that attracted customer dollars and plaudits in the press. The *Indianapolis Times*, reporting on the shopping center's upcoming opening, raved about "the exciting, dream-designed cluster of five future-flavored buildings, gay in nursery rhyme colors, on a fifty-five acre site," which would "usher in a new era of effortless shopping," and gushed over "the breathless beauty of the branch stores" of Ayres and Block's.[1] An additional advantage of suburban centers was that female shoppers were free to dress casually. A visit to the downtown flagship stores traditionally required women to don a hat and gloves. In a newspaper advertisement, Ayres made clear that at Glendale, one could "come as you are, shop in comfort, park with ease, [and] bring the children."[2] The outlying shopping center was, then, better adapted to the more casual, automobile-dominated, high-birthrate postwar era than were the stodgier downtown flagships, where parking was at a premium and a hatless woman without gloves was decidedly underdressed.

Originally both Eastgate and Glendale were open-air centers. By the late 1960s, however, the enclosed, climate-controlled shopping mall was transforming suburban retailing throughout the United States. Lafayette Square Mall, which opened in 1968 on the city's northwest side, was the first enclosed shopping center in the Indianapolis area. Larger than its open-air predecessors, it included a J. C. Penney's, a Sears, a movie theater, a Block's branch, and eventually an Ayres outlet. In 1972 the sprawling Castleton Square enclosed mall welcomed its first customers on the city's northeast side. At that time, it was the largest mall in Indiana and boasted a center court with a fountain, chandeliers, and planters lush with tropical vegetation. Perhaps most important, Castleton also offered parking for 7,050 automobiles. In 1974 Washington Square Mall opened on the city's far east side, draining business from the now-aging Eastgate Shopping Center just three miles to the west. With branches of Ayres and Block's, Washington Square conformed to the established mall pattern increasingly commonplace throughout the United States. Big-name anchor stores drew customers to the mall, and smaller chain stores supplemented the retail offering. Surrounding it all was the expansive parking lot, a ubiquitous feature of the automobile age.

In 1961 Ayres added a new element to the suburban scene when it launched the Ayr-Way discount store. Ayr-Way dispensed with the clerks who served customers in traditional department stores. Instead, its stores were self-service, with a checkout line similar to the established practice in supermarkets. The first Ayr-Way store on the city's northeast side proved a great success, attracting throngs of budget-conscious shoppers. On opening day, automobiles lined up for a mile waiting to get into the one-thousand-car parking lot. For once, a suburban retailer fell short in accommodating the ever-present automobile. This success encouraged Ayres management to launch other discount outlets in outlying areas of Indianapolis. A second store opened in 1962, followed by a south-side branch in 1963. Ayr-Way spread to other cities as well, and by 1969 the discount stores contributed more than one-third of the business of L.S. Ayres and Company.

The outward flow of population not only affected the material life of retailers but also redrew the spiritual map of Indianapolis. Just as Ayres and Block's sought locations closer to the homes of their customers, many of the city's religious institutions felt compelled to follow their parishioners to sites farther from the city center. New locations removed from the core proved more convenient to churchgoers and kept them in the pews on the Sabbath. Outlying sites also provided room for expansion and the all-important ample parking.

In 1947 the oldest Methodist congregation in the city abandoned its downtown building and merged with a north-side congregation. In 1952 these Methodists completed a new church building far up fashionable North Meridian Street. Long-established St. Paul's Episcopal Church, which had counted many prominent Indianapolis figures among its parishioners, built a new church in 1949 on North Meridian far to the north of its former downtown site. Joining the Methodists and Episcopalians in the migration northward was the Second Presbyterian Church. Its founding minister, Henry Ward Beecher, had established it as a powerful force in the spiritual life of the Indianapolis community. In 1959 this long-prominent congregation moved from downtown to a generous twenty-acre plot even farther north on Meridian than the churches of the Methodists and Episcopalians. Well-heeled Christians were not the only ones migrating northward and distancing themselves from the Mile Square. The city's Jewish population also found homes on the far north side. Following its members northward, in 1958 the Indianapolis Hebrew Congregation, the city's oldest Jewish congregation, moved to a new facility along affluent North Meridian. Both materially and spiritually, decentralization was the order of the day. Between 1945 and 1980, a powerful centrifugal force was transforming Indianapolis, drawing residents, retailers, and religious institutions ever outward.

Contributing to this centrifugal force was the opening of a network of interstate highways. In 1956 Congress passed the Federal-Aid Highway Act, which authorized the creation of a nationwide network of high-speed, limited-access freeways. Included in the plan for interstate highways were freeways designed to increase accessibility to downtown areas and funnel traffic to the business core. Central business districts had thrived in the

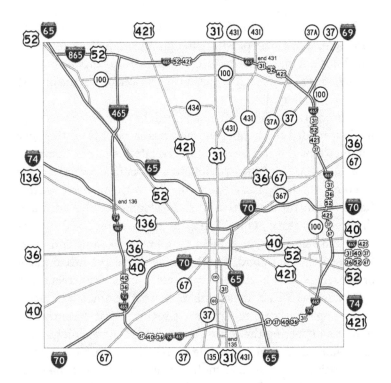

Interstate highways in the Indianapolis metro area

era of streetcar transportation, but restrictive city speed limits, as well as the traditional urban street pattern with frequent intersections, crosswalks, and bus and streetcar stops, deterred automobile-age Americans from traveling downtown. The urban interstates were expected to remedy these problems.

In fact, the opposite occurred. The interstates were more likely to funnel people outward than draw them inward. In Indianapolis, as elsewhere, outlying interstate routes became the new main streets as commerce congregated along the highways. The northern stretch of the Interstate 465 outer belt proved especially attractive to investors. A retail corridor developed from the Fashion Mall luxury shopping center, which opened in the early 1970s, to Castleton Square Mall three miles to the east. In coming years, drivers passing through Indianapolis would learn that I-465 north, which was intended to skirt the urban area, did not bypass the city's traffic. Instead, it serviced one of the busiest areas of Indianapolis.

Office parks proliferated along this highway, which was originally intended to channel through traffic away from the busy commerce of the city. In 1971 College Life Insurance Company broke ground for its office complex known as The Pyramids along the I-465 north bypass. Designed by the distinguished architect Kevin Roche, the distinctive office development was made up of three eleven-story pyramid-shaped structures encased in concrete and reflective glass. Sited on a green meadow and overlooking a tranquil pond, The Pyramids defied the urban norm of densely packed office structures along busy city streets. The Pyramids was a pastoral suburban alternative and a landmark, reminding drivers on the interstate highway that decentralization was impacting the office sector. The trio of buildings were much-lauded examples of modern architecture and won praise from critics across the nation. It was noteworthy that the most highly regarded local office development of the period from 1945 to 1975 was in far northern Marion County and not in the Mile Square.

The interstates not only attracted offices and malls but also enabled central Indiana residents to commute to homes farther from the core, exacerbating urban sprawl and decentralization. As the Indianapolis-area interstates began opening to traffic in the 1960s and 1970s, they primarily contributed to outward development rather than facilitated inward movement. Central Indiana residents were using them to move out of the city rather than as a means of transporting their consumer and investment dollars to the Mile Square. Ultimately, the interstate highways proved a drain on the central city and a boon to suburbanization.

Another factor in the decentralization of the city was the rise in air travel. Before 1945 railroads transported most travelers to

The Pyramids office building

the city. In the 1950s and 1960s, however, air travel boomed, and Indianapolis's airport, located on the far western edge of Marion County, became the major point entry for millions of passengers. From 1955 to 1965, passenger traffic at the Indianapolis airport rose 99 percent from 610,000 to 1,215,000. By 1970 there were more than one million people arriving by air and another one million departing. People coming to the city no longer stepped out of the doors of Union Station within walking distance of

Monument Circle, the statehouse, and Ayres. Instead, in increasingly decentralized Indianapolis, they came and went from a new hub of intercity transportation on the far west side.

Though the forces of decentralization seemed inexorable, spawning new outlying hubs of transport, residence, and business, Indianapolis was not succumbing wholly to the powerful centrifugal forces transforming metropolitan America. In 1969 city leaders secured state legislative approval of a reform scheme, popularly dubbed Unigov, that would in large part thwart political decentralization. The Committee on Postwar Planning had feared that dreaded decentralization would lead to a city surrounded by a Chinese wall of independent and often uncooperative suburban governments. Other midwestern cities, such as Cleveland, Cincinnati, and Saint Louis, had suffered this fate, which blocked their further growth. Unigov, however, limited the possibility of debilitating city-suburban clashes by consolidating the governments of the city of Indianapolis and Marion County. Under this reform plan, there would be a single mayor for the city and county, and a twenty-nine-member city-county council would serve as the legislative branch of the expanded metropolis. The scheme centralized governmental authority, placing countywide policymaking in the hands of public officials working out of the downtown city-county building. Under Unigov, local governments within Marion County would not enclose Indianapolis in a Chinese wall, and a multitude of suburban municipalities would not proliferate in outlying county areas. Unigov marked the triumph of centralization over decentralization.

Contrary to its name, Unigov did not, however, consolidate all governments in the county. The nine township governments survived, as did the township fire departments. Moreover, it did not consolidate the city police department with the county sheriff's office. Perhaps most important, Unigov preserved the eleven independent school districts. Residents of the outlying townships remained outside the Indianapolis Public Schools district. In addition, four existing suburban municipalities, Speedway, Beech Grove, Southport, and Lawrence, retained their independence.

They were not part of the enlarged city of Indianapolis. Basically, Unigov preserved much of the existing governmental fragmentation but blocked any further dispersion of authority among suburban units.

Though not providing total consolidation, Unigov did radically enlarge the population and tax base of the city of Indianapolis. In 1960 the federal census counted 476,258 residents in the city of Indianapolis; it ranked twenty-sixth in population among American cities. In the 1970 census, after the adoption of Unigov, Indianapolis rose to the rank of eleventh, with a population of 744,674. Moreover, as a result of Unigov, the city's area increased from 82 square miles to 368 square miles, meaning the newly consolidated city had room to grow. These were figures that brought joy to any chamber of commerce booster. Indianapolis, unlike many other older cities, was not doomed to become a shrinking, decaying hub cut off from growth by an independent suburbia. Unigov had thus partially mitigated the ill effects of an outwardly expanding population. Indianapolis was not choked by suburbs. Instead, it swallowed them.

Whereas the consolidated city as a whole was growing, much of Indianapolis was suffering distress and decline. To meet the rising demand for housing during the war years and in the late 1940s, landlords divided the large Victorian homes on the near north side into apartments. The wealthy kept moving northward, leaving the lower reaches of Meridian, Pennsylvania, and Delaware Streets to renters. In the 1950s and early 1960s, there was little appreciation for houses with turrets, front porches, and gingerbread trim. They were remnants of what seemed a benighted past. Consequently, some were demolished, and others housed residents who could not afford more modern accommodations. As yet there was no mass enthusiasm for historic neighborhoods. In midcentury Indianapolis, the prevailing mantra seemed to be the newer the better.

Moreover, the construction of the interstate highways had required the destruction of swaths of inner-city housing, with dire consequences for some older neighborhoods. An estimated seventeen thousand people were displaced as interstate highway construction leveled housing in Indianapolis. Those residents who were not displaced had to suffer the noise and vibrations generated by the new highways running through their neighborhoods. Residents affected by the highway plans protested, but the cycle of destruction and construction proceeded. Interstate 70 cut through the heart of the working-class Near Southside neighborhood, isolating residents north of the highway from neighborhood churches and homes located south of the freeway. The interstates made downtown accessible to suburban dwellers but rendered some sections of older neighborhoods inaccessible to residents who lived a few blocks away.

Meanwhile, downtown Indianapolis was showing signs of age and losing its edge to newer developments along the metropolitan fringe. Retail data revealed a gradual leakage of consumer dollars from the city's core. In 1948 downtown stores accounted for nearly 45 percent of retail sales in the metropolitan area; by 1958 this figure had fallen to 37 percent. Moreover, downtown merchants feared the decline was irreversible. At the opening ceremony of the Glendale Shopping Center, the assistant manager of the Washington Street Ayres flagship was heard to say, "This is the beginning of the end of the downtown store."[3]

During the 1950s and 1960s, the giant Ayres and Block's emporiums downtown continued to attract shoppers and were not yet failing. By the 1970s, however, there were serious signs of decay along the premier retailing expanse of Washington Street. In 1973 a spectacular fire destroyed the building that had housed the W. T. Grant store on Washington Street and caused irreparable damage to the adjoining Thomas office building. In the wake of the fire, both buildings were leveled, and the site became a parking lot. The lot was expected to exist only temporarily, pending future development. But this temporary void in the street frontage of the city's chief retailing thoroughfare survived well into the twenty-first century. During the early twentieth century, businesses vied for a location on Washington Street, and the prospect of high rental income ensured that investors would not leave any empty lots in the prime shopping district. By 1973, however, economic realities had changed. Downtown was not necessarily the optimal place to invest one's dollars.

Other developments seemed to tell the same story of gradual decline. In 1974 the Kresge store closed, even though it enjoyed an enviable location next to the Ayres flagship. For the following twenty years, the building at this formerly prime site remained vacant. Then, in 1979, the H. P. Wasson store, across the street from Ayres, closed, the first of Indianapolis's big three department stores to go out of business. The Ayres and Block's downtown outlets lingered on until the early 1990s, depending on a dwindling clientele whose loyalty was fueled by nostalgic memories of genteel tearooms and lavish Christmas displays.

In 1975 a survey of Indianapolis architecture commented on the depressing change. "Today the area around and including Washington Street is but a shadow of its former self," it reported. "What stores remain cater to a less-affluent clientele. Huge gaping holes exist in the street facade." According to this account, "The teaming crowds are gone, and the streets look deserted at 6:00 p.m. . . . Window shopping along the street is almost a lost art." Describing the secondary downtown shopping district along Massachusetts Avenue, the survey concluded, "The street manages to stay alive, just barely, but it has all the characteristics of a 'Skid Row' [with] boarded store fronts, vacant lots and raucous bars."[4] By the 1970s downtown Indianapolis was clearly in need of a major boost to bring it out of its prevailing doldrums.

Adding to the grim picture were the closures of major downtown hotels. During the 1940s, 1950s, and 1960s, no new first-class hotels were built in downtown Indianapolis. Instead, the aging hotels constructed in the early twentieth century continued to serve travelers. As passenger rail traffic dwindled to a trickle by the late 1960s, downtown hotels clustered a short distance from Union Station suffered. Auto-borne travelers preferred newer outlying motels designed to accommodate cars.

The older hotels in the core could handle convention goers and commercial travelers, but they seemed off the path of many visitors to the city.

The Claypool Hotel had dominated the downtown lodging business since its opening in 1903, but it was losing its luster as a grand hostelry by midcentury. Two sensational murders of young women in the Claypool, one in 1943 and the other in 1954, had received national attention and brought unwanted notoriety to the hotel. In 1954 accounts of the eighteen-year-old victim found stuffed in a dresser drawer especially titillated scandal-hungry Americans. A fire in 1967 sealed the fate of the hotel, and the building was demolished two years later. Its site on a prime corner of Washington Street remained vacant for more than a decade, another stark reminder of the decline of the city's once-preeminent thoroughfare.

Other downtown hotels also went out of business. In 1963 the Hotel Washington closed; its general manager attributed the Washington's fate to competition from new outlying motels, which had been eroding the hotel's business for a number of years. The Lincoln Hotel, which had become a Sheraton in 1955, surrendered to the changing times in 1970, further reducing the inventory of downtown accommodations. During the 1970s the opening of some new hotels offered the promise of a brighter future, but as yet it was not clear whether the Mile Square would ever revive as a destination for visitors and their cash.

By the 1970s, however, there seemed little hope for downtown movie palaces. During the 1950s the popularity of drive-in theaters diverted many auto-borne cinema lovers from the older movie venues. In later years new theaters at outlying shopping malls increased the competition facing downtown movie houses. Perhaps most damaging to the motion picture business was the advent of television. Indianapolis's first television station began broadcasting in 1949, and during the following eight years, the addition of three more stations expanded the entertainment options of central Indiana audiences. As early as 1953, more than 139,000 television sets brought programming to the living rooms of Indianapolis-area residents. As the number of sets increased, Hoosiers could enjoy entertainment without having to get into their cars and go to a drive-in and certainly without having to make the trek downtown and buy a ticket at one of the movie palaces built in the prewar era.

One after another, the downtown theaters closed. In 1969 the once highly touted Lyric Theater went out of business and soon after was demolished to make way for a parking garage. The Loew's Theatre closed in 1970, and the opulent Indiana Theatre on Washington Street presented its last film in 1975. The Circle Theatre continued to show movies until 1981, but following its demise as a movie venue, there was no first-run cinema in the central business district for fourteen years. The big screens went dark, but both the Indiana and the Circle escaped the wrecking ball. The Indiana became the home of the Indiana Repertory Theatre, presenting live performances, and the Circle survived as the home of the Indianapolis Symphony Orchestra.

Another casualty of the changing times was public transit. Wartime rationing of gasoline and tires had forced thousands of Indianapolis residents to rely on streetcars and buses for trips to work or to the store. After the war, however, they readily abandoned their place on the bus for a seat behind the wheel of the latest automobile. According to the transit company's annual report for 1951, automobile registrations in the Indianapolis area had risen 41 percent over the previous five years, and the number of passengers using public transit had dropped 28 percent. This same trend continued over the following two decades. Bus patronage fell as auto use rose. By 1970, 84 percent of Indianapolis residents relied on private automobiles to get to work, while only 7.5 percent commuted by bus. Ten years later, the share traveling to work by bus had fallen even further to 4.8 percent. Nine out of every ten went to work in private vehicles. The automobile was triumphant, with public transit serving primarily those too poor to buy a car or those miscreants who had lost their driver's license. Few people seemed to prefer public transit. If they were able, they traveled by car.

This change was bad news for the beleaguered downtown. Mile Square institutions had thrived in the streetcar era when transit lines converged on downtown, funneling customers to the pre-eminent business district. Before the automobile era, movement was largely restricted to the streetcar lines. A person could not head in any direction but basically could only travel where the streetcar lines went. Yet behind the wheel of an automobile, an Indianapolis resident could go wherever there were roads, and a driver could more readily travel to a shopping mall than to the central business district. Moreover, he or she could travel faster than on a streetcar or a bus. During the mid-twentieth century, the automobile enabled the people of central Indiana to move outward to new residences on the metropolitan fringe and to spend their money at outlying shopping centers and drive-in theaters. But interstates carrying a growing number of vehicles destroyed thousands of homes, parking lots left gaping holes in the street frontage of Washington Street, and parking garages replaced once-grand theaters. The automobile had facilitated both the expansion and the decline of the city.

RACIAL CHANGE AND CONFLICT

One rapidly growing element of postwar Indianapolis was the African American community. The city's expanding job market during the 1940s attracted thousands of Blacks from the South. Indianapolis's African American population increased from 51,000 in 1940 to 64,000 in 1950, and the Black share of the city's total population rose from 13 percent to 15 percent. The increase was even more dramatic in the 1950s. During that decade there was a remarkable 54 percent rise in the city's Black population as the number of African Americans increased to 98,000, or 21 percent of the total number of Indianapolis residents. Owing to the adoption of Unigov and the absorption of the largely white suburban population, the figure fell to 18 percent in 1970. Migration from the South slowed in the 1970s, but by 2000 there were 199,000 Blacks living in Indianapolis, constituting one-fourth of all residents.

As the Black population rose, entrenched practices of racial exclusion gradually disappeared. In 1949 the Indiana legislature adopted a school desegregation law, abandoning the state's long-standing acceptance of separate schools for Blacks and whites. During the 1950s the number of African Americans in Indianapolis's formerly all-white high schools increased. After a quarter century of racial segregation, Blacks could once again attend prestigious Shortridge High School. Crispus Attucks High School survived, however, and its student body remained 100 percent Black. By the close of the 1950s, the traditionally white high schools were integrated but the Black high school remained segregated. Education at Crispus Attucks remained separate but in one regard decidedly better than equal. In 1955 Crispus Attucks won the state high school basketball championship, the first Indianapolis high to do so. It again secured the championship in 1956 and 1959, triumphing in a sport Hoosiers held in near-sacred esteem.

Meanwhile, the local chapter of the NAACP was acting to challenge racial discrimination. In 1947 Indianapolis Blacks organized the "eating crusade." Armed with copies of Indiana's rarely enforced civil rights law, adopted in the late nineteenth century, African Americans sought service at downtown lunch counters and restaurants and made clear to reluctant establishments that exclusion on the basis of race was illegal. The persistent challenges reaped some results. In 1950 a prominent figure in the fight for change reported to the NAACP national office that "direct action to open restaurants etc. [was] succeeding in forcing compliance with the Indiana Civil Rights Law in many restaurants, hotels and theaters." According to this activist, "The Indianapolis hotels recently opened their doors to Negro members of the National Bar Association, Veterans of Foreign Wars, CIO, etc." He admitted, "Much discrimination in these accommodations still exists [but] the Association program is steadily winning on all fronts."[5]

By the 1960s downtown Indianapolis was no longer a white preserve with Blacks consigned to their own turf along Indiana Avenue. In 1963 Indiana lawmakers adopted a new, more stringent civil rights act with an enforcement mechanism to ensure an end to racial segregation in such public accommodations as hotels and restaurants. It created a state civil rights commission charged with implementing the law, and Governor Matthew Welsh issued an executive order that mandated that Indiana licensing agencies require compliance from hotels, motels, bars, and eating places operating under state licenses

Not only were Blacks now booking rooms at downtown hotels and eating at formerly all-white restaurants, they were gradually moving out of the old neighborhoods and finding homes in areas once reserved for whites. As they moved north from the Indiana Avenue area, they faced resistance, but the expanding Black population continued to push outward. During World War II, white residents of the North Indianapolis Civic League dedicated themselves to preventing any Blacks from moving into the area extending from Twenty-Eighth to Thirty-Eighth Streets. Yet by 1957 an estimated 87 percent of the residents living in the neighborhood from Twenty-Eighth to Thirty-Fourth Streets were African American, and for the area between Thirty-Fourth and Thirty-Eighth Streets, the figure was an estimated 75 percent. Block-busting real estate agents sought to convince white homeowners, panic stricken by fear of falling property values, to move out of areas on the verge of racial transition. Taking advantage of white fears, real estate agents bought the houses at below market value and then sold them, for much-inflated prices, to incoming Blacks eager to find dwellings.

Some neighborhoods, however, sought to end this cycle of panic selling. In 1956 residents of the area north of Thirty-Eighth Street formed the Butler-Tarkington Neighborhood Association to ensure a stable racial mix in the area and create a community in which whites would remain and Blacks were welcome. They proved successful, maintaining a racial balance throughout the remainder of the century and forestalling the racial tensions that usually arose when African Americans moved into white areas.

Some affluent African Americans were moving farther out to the suburban fringes, where they built new homes rather than settle for older dwellings handed down by fleeing whites. The Grandview community, in a prestigious area of Washington Township northwest of the city, developed into a residential refuge for Indianapolis's most successful African Americans. In 1955 developers began marketing the eighty-eight-lot Augusta Way subdivision in the Grandview area, claiming that it offered "a new opportunity for country living with all of the city conveniences." Advertisements for Augusta Way boasted of "reasonable restrictions," implying that this was not a place where potential buyers would have to mix with the city's less successful African Americans. In 1966 a columnist in the city's African American newspaper described the Grandview area as a "golden ghetto" and as the "new sepia heaven" where "hundreds of Negroes live[d] in . . . showplace homes." It was a reservation for "many of the Negroes who ha[d] struck it rich . . . in the post war economy" and "decided to escape the ghetto by building split-level and ranch type homes out in the suburbs."[6]

Despite the presence of some affluent Blacks in Washington Township, the outlying areas of Marion County remained overwhelmingly white. Consequently, the adoption of Unigov in 1969 and the absorption of the fringe townships into the city changed the composition of Indianapolis's population and the prevailing balance of political power. Since the 1930s, Democrats had usually prevailed in Indianapolis city elections. Of the fourteen mayors serving from 1930 through 1967, eleven were Democrats and only three were Republicans. During this same period, African Americans abandoned the party of Lincoln and became staunch supporters of Democrat candidates. Moreover, by the late 1960s, Blacks accounted for about 27 percent of Indianapolis's residents and were nearly half of the Democratic Party's base electorate in the city. African Americans, then, were approaching majority status within the city's majority party and seemed poised to achieve significant political power in the city and someday capture the office of mayor.

In 1967, however, Indianapolis elected the Republican Richard Lugar as mayor, and the following year, the GOP won the state governor's office and majorities in both houses of the state legislature. The Republicans were in total control and exploited their good fortune by adopting Unigov, which added tens of thousands of white Republican voters living in suburban areas to the city's electorate. With these new voters, Indianapolis would be safely Republican, and Blacks would become a diminished voting bloc.

In response, Democrats denounced the reform, labeling it "Unigrab," and some prominent Blacks joined in the criticism. One Black political leader attacked Unigov as "dangerous and maliciously motivated as to race and a political enslavement of minorities and an unfair power grab."[7] Not all Indianapolis Blacks were so alarmed, but many were wary of the reform. In a front-page article headlined "Negroes Oppose Lugar Unigov Plan," Indianapolis's Black newspaper reported on criticism of the scheme in the Black community. Some Black opponents seemed to believe that the principal "purpose of the measure was to eliminate the possibility of a Negro being elected mayor at some future date as happened [in] Gary." As one critic observed, "Practical politics now dictates that political aspirants in Indianapolis . . . make definite overtures to the Negro community." Unigov, however, "would preclude the necessity for any special concern for problems confronting the Negro," and it was "theoretically possible that matters of extreme importance to the Negro [might] well be abandoned."[8] Put simply, Blacks would not count for as much politically if thousands of white suburbanites were added to the voting rolls.

The new form of government did offer some advantages to Blacks. Prior to Unigov, city council members were elected at large, meaning that Black neighborhoods had no direct representation. The white-dominated political parties slated Black candidates in the expectation that at least one would win. Yet African American winners did not owe their election solely to Black neighborhood voters but secured victory because of their acceptability to the predominantly white at-large electorate. Under Unigov, the city-county council consisted of twenty-five members elected by districts and four at-large members. District representation meant that candidates from Black neighborhoods were now ensured seats on the council no matter what the majority-white, at-large electorate thought.

As Democrats feared, however, Unigov certainly forestalled Democrat victory at the polls. Republicans held the mayor's office throughout the remainder of the twentieth century. Under Unigov, African Americans were a minority in the electorate and adherents to the minority political party. Unlike many large cities across the nation, Indianapolis would not elect a Black mayor during the half century following Unigov's adoption. For the time being, Indianapolis was a white Republican stronghold.

Debate over the merits of Unigov was dividing the local political scene, but most Indianapolis whites seemed pleased with the relatively harmonious nature of race relations in the capital city. Angry Blacks rioted in cities across the nation during the hot summers of the 1960s, and following the assassination of Martin Luther King Jr. in April 1968, civil disorder swept the nation. Indianapolis, however, remained peaceful. In December 1968 the *Indianapolis Sunday Star Magazine* published an article titled "The Indianapolis Formula for Racial Peace." "There is something astonishing and marvelous about Indianapolis," wrote the author of the article. "It is the only city remotely near its size in the North . . . that hasn't had a single racial disturbance."[9] He admitted that relations between the Black community and the police might be tense, but overall, the author congratulated Indianapolis on its handling of the race issue.

Only six months later, in June 1969, violence erupted in the Lockefield Place neighborhood, which proved that the Indianapolis formula for racial peace was not as effective as self-congratulatory whites had assumed. When two police officers responded to a call regarding an alleged fight in the neighborhood, many African Americans were already seething with anger because of the recent conviction of Black Panther activists for burglary and conspiracy to murder. Twenty young Black males ambushed the responding officers, and a crowd of about three hundred area residents gathered and proceeded to pelt the police reinforcements with bottles and bricks. Gunfire resulted in the wounding of one police officer, and another officer suffered a beating. Two days of rioting followed. Protesters looted and damaged area businesses, and a gasoline-ignited fire destroyed the local supermarket. More than one hundred rioters were arrested. Clearly, Indianapolis was not a peaceful exception to the American rule of volatile race relations. In the Hoosier capital, as elsewhere, a state of cold war seemed to exist between African Americans and the police.

During the 1970s, however, the dominant racial issue in Indianapolis was not police relations but desegregation of the public schools. In 1968 the United States Justice Department filed a suit charging the board of the Indianapolis Public Schools with failing to desegregate its schools. The board had perpetuated racial segregation by drawing the boundaries of school attendance zones to ensure that some schools remained overwhelmingly Black while others were predominantly white. In 1971 federal district court judge S. Hugh Dillin upheld the Justice Department complaint, ruling that the city's school system had engaged in de jure segregation. During the following decade, litigation over the issue remained bogged down in the federal courts as the Indianapolis school authorities and the state of Indiana appealed Dillin's decision. Unigov also became a point of contention. The parties seeking desegregation claimed that the framers of Unigov had failed to consolidate the suburban township school districts with the Indianapolis district in order to allay suburban fears of racial integration. The preservation of independent suburban township districts was, then, further evidence of official action to segregate, and consequently the suburban districts needed to be part of a court-ordered solution. To remedy the situation, Judge Dillin ordered the busing of African American students from the Indianapolis Public Schools district to the suburban school districts, and in 1981 the transfer of nearly seven thousand Black students to the outer township schools began. In some cities, most notably Boston, busing to achieve racial balance ignited heated protests by angry white parents and students. In Indianapolis, some parents grumbled and complained, and there were minor clashes, but the implementation of the program was relatively peaceful.

Meanwhile, relations between the Black community and the police remained tense. Police brutality and targeting of young Black males were persistent complaints, and some well-publicized incidents lent credence to African American charges of police bias. Perhaps the most notable incident was the shooting death of Michael Taylor in 1987. Police arrested the sixteen-year-old Taylor on suspicion of auto theft. He was placed in the back seat of a police car with his hands cuffed behind him. When the squad car arrived at the Marion County Juvenile Center, he was found with a fatal bullet wound in his head. The police claimed it was suicide, the despondent teenager having shot himself with a gun hidden in his sneakers. The coroner agreed, as did other investigators called in to examine the controversial case. Many in the Black community, however, believed the suicide explanation was one more example of a police cover-up. Demonstrators marched to police headquarters to protest what they believed was racially motivated murder. "You have to have lived here for the last 20 years to understand this incident as it relates to the black community," explained a local civil rights activist. "Historically we are suspicious. This opens old wounds." Summing up the feelings of African Americans in the capital city, he concluded, "The problem in Indianapolis . . . is that blacks are tolerated but not accepted."[10]

Nine years later a civil suit brought by Taylor's family against the city of Indianapolis reopened the issue. In 1996 an all-white jury awarded the Taylor family $4.3 million in damages, rejecting the suicide claim. But the city continued to insist that the teenager killed himself, and the case remained a subject of speculation and controversy. It was incontrovertible, however, that the Taylor incident widened the divide between Indianapolis Blacks and the police department.

In 1992 Mayor Stephen Goldsmith sought to heal the rift by appointing James D. Toler as Indianapolis's first Black police chief. It seemed a conciliatory act by the white Republican mayor. Yet at the close of the century, police practices remained the principal cause of racial unrest in the city, and Toler's appointment could not allay a long history of suspicion or close old wounds. Over the previous half century, Black-white relations had changed markedly. African Americans were no longer consigned to an Indiana Avenue ghetto. They could eat in any restaurant or stay at any hotel. Despite Unigov, they enjoyed increased political clout, and a growing number were joining the outward migration to Marion County's fringe townships. By 1990 only 34 percent of the county's Blacks lived in Center Township, while 39 percent resided in the two northern townships of Washington and Lawrence. Indianapolis had changed. The Michael Taylor case and persistent complaints about police brutality, however, exposed a lasting legacy of distrust and division.

REVITALIZATION

In the 1940s, 1950s, and 1960s, older cities of the Northeast and Midwest realized they needed to meet the emerging challenge of suburbia and the threatening competition from growing Sunbelt metropolises. Wealth, population, and jobs were moving from the older urban core to the metropolitan fringe and to rapidly developing cities in the South, which offered a warmer climate, a union-free workforce, and business-friendly governments. Consequently, the leaders of aging northern cities embraced urban renewal schemes aimed at clearing slums and creating a new built environment of sleek, glass-encased high-rises. Older cities sought to shed the drab attire of the past and don a fresh look that would proclaim to the world that they were not over the hill. Federal urban renewal money was supposed to facilitate this transformation as Washington joined with officials in city halls to bring aging hubs back to life.

Indianapolis leaders recognized the signs of decline in the urban core, yet unlike in other cities in the Northeast and Midwest, both public and private sector leaders rejected federal aid throughout the 1950s and early 1960s. Intervention from Washington was anathema to many city officials and was especially odious to powerful chamber of commerce executive president William Book. As a result, Indianapolis lagged in the implementation of revitalization initiatives and could not match the achievements of urban renewal stars such as Pittsburgh and New Haven, Connecticut.

When John Barton assumed the mayor's office in 1964, he recognized the need to act. In 1965 he organized the Greater Indianapolis Progress Committee, an advisory body of civic and business leaders that promoted projects for the improvement and revitalization of the city. A powerful force in the coming years, the committee mobilized influential figures from the private sector in support of public sector initiatives. Deviating from past practices, Barton also sought federal funding and reactivated the city's public housing program.

Despite his achievements, the Democrat Barton suffered defeat when seeking reelection, ceding the office of mayor to the Republican Richard Lugar. Lugar assumed an even more activist role than Barton, relying on the Greater Indianapolis Progress Committee to further a revitalization agenda. Unigov, Lugar's crowning achievement, boosted Indianapolis's reputation nationwide and won the Hoosier capital accolades as a city on the rise. Through Unigov, Indianapolis had severed its suburban noose, a goal envied by cities throughout the Northeast and Midwest. It had achieved what other cities had failed to do and seemed to be a city that could realize extraordinary ends.

During Lugar's administration, there were other signs of new life in the city. In 1968 Lugar urged the creation of a great state university in Indianapolis. For a number of years, both Indiana University and Purdue University had offered extension courses in the city, and the Indiana University medical school had established a campus northeast of Monument Circle in the early twentieth century. Yet there was no comprehensive state university campus in the capital city. Responding to Lugar's call for action, the two major state institutions of higher education merged their Indianapolis programs to form Indiana University Purdue University Indianapolis (IUPUI) in 1969. Over the succeeding decades, a complex of university buildings arose adjacent to the medical school facilities as the new university attracted an increasing body of students and its expanding corps of employees boosted the city's economy.

Construction cranes further announced the reawakening of the Mile Square. In 1970 Indiana National Bank completed construction of the thirty-six-story INB Tower, which soared 504 feet above the downtown and would remain the city's tallest building throughout the 1970s. The sleek aluminum, glass, and marble structure advertised that Indianapolis was shedding its relatively low-rise past and developing a skyline worthy of a major city. That same year a new Hilton hotel opened in the Mile Square, filling a void left by the closure of the venerable hostelries that had dominated the downtown lodging scene for decades.

More significant was the opening of a downtown convention center in 1972. Deemed a high priority by the Greater Indianapolis Progress Committee, the new convention center enabled the Hoosier capital to host larger meetings and attract a growing number of free-spending convention goers to the city's core. The center proved so successful that it was necessary to expand the facility in 1984 and 1992–1993. During the final decades of the twentieth century, the convention center was a looming symbol of renewed vitality and a reminder that a mounting wave of visitors was converging on the once-distressed downtown.

In 1974 the opening of Market Square Arena was another sign that downtown was not dead. With seating for seventeen thousand spectators, Market Square, at the time of its completion, was the fifth-largest sports arena in America. It was the home of the Indiana Pacers professional basketball team and the Indianapolis Racers hockey team. In addition, it was a leading concert venue, most notably hosting Elvis Presley's last live performance seven weeks before his death in 1977. And Billy Graham held a massive revival there in 1980. Like the convention center, the arena drew people to the central business district. Because of Market Square, Indianapolis's downtown was a destination for thousands of fans of basketball and rock and roll, as well as Hoosiers seeking spiritual uplift.

An additional encouraging landmark was the Merchants Plaza complex, located on the site of the demolished Lincoln Hotel. Under construction from 1974 to 1977, it was composed of two fifteen-story office towers and a 535-room Hyatt Regency Hotel. The hotel's dramatic nineteen-story atrium and revolving circular restaurant on the twentieth floor distinguished it as a major downtown attraction. It was a luxury hotel that seemed to mark Indianapolis as a place that could accommodate the most discriminating travelers. Moreover, it was an encouraging portent of a possibly better future for the city's central business district.

While Merchants Plaza was under construction, Richard Lugar stepped down as mayor and was succeeded by a man who embodied the spirit of the city's renaissance. William Hudnut served as mayor of Indianapolis for sixteen years, from 1976 through 1991, and more than any previous mayor left his mark on the city. Born in Cincinnati and educated at Princeton and the Union Theological Seminary in New York City, Hudnut came to Indianapolis to serve as pastor of the prestigious Second Presbyterian Church. He left the pulpit when elected to the United States House of Representatives. He was not, however, done with preaching. As mayor he preached the gospel of urban revival, and his evangelical fervor won thousands of converts in his adopted hometown. He was unequaled as an urban cheerleader with a remarkable ability to convince his fellow citizens to join in his crusade to transform Indianapolis. His enthusiasm and unbounded faith in the city were contagious, and his charismatic personality helped secure his repeated reelection by landslide majorities.

Most notably, Hudnut sought to create a positive image for Indianapolis. He claimed that the city was known for the Indianapolis 500 race and little else. It did not register on the American mind. Sometimes derided as Naptown, the supposedly sleepy Hoosier capital lacked a reputation that could draw investors and visitors and promote general economic development. Hudnut never tired of announcing that his goal was to transform

"India-NO-place" into "India-SHOW-place." Indianapolis had to make itself known as a world-class city, a showplace worthy of the attention of people throughout the nation, if not the world. Throughout his long tenure as mayor, Hudnut preached that the city needed to establish an identity and become a place no one could ignore.

Mayor Hudnut believed that partnership between government and the private sector was essential to the revitalization of Indianapolis. He worked closely with the preexisting Greater Indianapolis Progress Committee and encouraged the creation of a number of private, not-for-profit bodies that were expected to help achieve his dream of an energized metropolis. The Corporate Community Council, organized in 1977, was composed of the chief executive officers of major Indianapolis businesses and included the mayor and governor as ex officio members. Its purpose was to mobilize the corporate community behind the initiatives for fashioning a greater city. That same year Indianapolis Downtown Inc. was founded to promote the revitalization of the central business district. Then, in 1979, business and government leaders joined to establish the Indiana Sports Corporation, charged with realizing Mayor Hudnut's goal of making Indianapolis a sports capital. Created in 1983, the Indianapolis Economic Development Corporation worked to promote business growth in the capital city. Its board included representatives of both the public and private sectors, and it operated under a contract with the city government. Indianapolis Project was incorporated in 1983, serving as the public relations arm of Indianapolis's revitalization campaign. It was to spread the good word of the city's success.

Though each of these were private organizations, they served to further the Hudnut administration's program. In his retrospective account of Indianapolis's transformation, Hudnut repeatedly stated how "we" established the technically private bodies.[11] In other words, the public sector mayor and private sector leaders were working in tandem, acting together to pursue a common end. The line between public and private became so blurred that the mayor could conflate them in a common "we."

The twin pillars of Hudnut's program to create a greater city were sports and downtown development. By becoming a major sports venue, Indianapolis would draw the attention of people throughout the nation. Millions of sports fans would not be able to ignore a city that hosted major contests and events. Indianapolis would appear on television screens across the country, and its name would become etched in the minds of sports enthusiasts. A renewed central business district would also ensure a new and better image for Indianapolis. Hudnut believed that cities were judged by their downtowns. A city with a shabby core and an uninspiring skyline was deemed a loser in the ranks of American cities. Soaring new high-rises, luxury hotels, a bustling downtown workforce, reenergized retailing, and a growing number of visitors and convention attendees were marks of urban greatness. Indianapolis's downtown needed to become a showplace to prove to the world that Naptown had awakened and become one of the nation's most alert cities.

Amateur athletics were the focus of the Hudnut-era sports initiative. In 1982 Indianapolis established itself as a significant player in the world of amateur athletics when it hosted the National Sports Festival. To prepare for the event, the Lilly Endowment provided financial support for the construction of a natatorium, a track-and-field stadium, and a bicycle-racing track. During the eight-day festival, more than 2,500 American athletes competed before a total of 250,000 spectators. Five years later Indianapolis cemented its reputation as an amateur sports venue when it was the site of the Pan American Games. Second only to the Olympics as a multisport event, the Pan American Games was deemed a crowning achievement in Indianapolis's campaign to achieve recognition. Eighty thousand spectators attended the opening ceremonies staged by Walt Disney Productions. It claimed to be the largest outdoor live show ever produced in the United States. There followed three weeks of competition by athletes from throughout the Western Hemisphere. CBS televised the event, ensuring that millions of viewers throughout the nation would know of Indianapolis's role in the sports world. Moreover, more than two thousand journalists reported on Indianapolis's triumphal games.

The Hudnut administration and its allies also sought to attract the headquarters of amateur sports organizations to Indianapolis. In 1970 the Amateur Athletic Union established its headquarters in the city, and during the Hudnut years, other amateur sports organizations followed suit. The governing bodies for track and field, gymnastics, synchronized swimming, rowing, baseball, canoeing and kayaking, and water polo all located in Indianapolis between 1981 and 1990. By the latter date, Indianapolis could plausibly boast of being not only the capital of Indiana but the amateur sports capital of America.

Hudnut, however, was not satisfied with simply attracting amateur sports events. He believed that Indianapolis had to establish itself on the national scene by hosting major-league professional sports teams. It was already home to the major-league Indiana Pacers basketball franchise, but a professional football team would supposedly ensure Indianapolis's entry into the ranks of America's leading cities. The construction of a facility to accommodate a professional team was deemed a prerequisite for achieving this big-league status. In 1982 the city broke ground for the Hoosier Dome, a sixty-thousand-seat multipurpose stadium linked to the downtown convention center. The public and private sectors jointly financed its construction. The Lilly Endowment contributed $25 million, and a city revenue bond would provide an additional $47.5 million. A 1 percent levy on restaurant and bar sales in Marion County would finance the debt on the bond. Indianapolis's new stadium was designed to host amateur sports contests and provide additional space for large conventions and trade shows, but on completion in 1984, it was also a potential venue for professional football.

Meanwhile, Robert Irsay, the owner of the Baltimore Colts football team, was deeply dissatisfied with both Baltimore's

New downtown skyline, post-1990

fans and its football stadium. With characteristic energy, Mayor Hudnut intervened and convinced Irsay to abandon Baltimore and move his team to Indianapolis. Fearful that the city of Baltimore would seize the franchise through eminent domain, in March 1984 Irsay packed up the Colts' belongings and moved out of Maryland in the middle of the night. Moving vans owned by Indianapolis-based Mayflower Transit facilitated the surreptitious departure. Baltimore fans were livid, but they had to accept Indianapolis's triumph. By 1984 Indianapolis was home to both major-league football and basketball teams. Moreover, both of them played downtown. Thus, Hudnut's sports strategy dovetailed with his downtown initiative. The Hoosier Dome and Market Square Arena ensured that the central business district was also a central sports destination. If one wanted to attend a major-league game in Indianapolis, one had to go downtown.

Yet sports facilities alone were not sufficient to create a revitalized Mile Square. Mayor Hudnut also sought to ensure that businesses would locate downtown and make it truly a district central to Indianapolis's business life. For example, city officials worked for months to forge a deal that would convince American United Life Insurance Company to build their new headquarters downtown rather than in the suburbs. To accommodate the company's need for space, the Hudnut administration helped assemble twenty-seven property parcels, vacated a part of Indiana Avenue, and arranged to move a sewer. The city's efforts seemed justified when the insurance company's new headquarters opened in 1982. It rose thirty-eight stories, 533 feet, and ranked as the tallest building in the city throughout the 1980s.

Other new structures soon transformed the Mile Square skyline. Six downtown office buildings of over twenty stories were completed during the three-year period from 1987 through 1989. Market Tower, 300 North Meridian, and First Indiana Place each soared over four hundred feet above the city sidewalks. In 1990 the completion of the 811-foot Bank One Tower literally overshadowed the city's other new skyscrapers and stole from the American United Life building the title of Indianapolis's tallest structure. By 1990 Indianapolis had a downtown skyline that advertised its big-city status. With a professional football team and gleaming new high-rises, Indianapolis seemed to realize Mayor Hudnut's definition of a dynamic city.

Downtown Indianapolis, however, lacked a reinvigorated retail sector. The flagship Ayres and Block's stores were on the verge of closing after years of declining sales. Washington Street no longer attracted crowds of shoppers, and it testified to decline rather than vitality. This was unacceptable in Mayor Hudnut's Indianapolis. To remedy the situation, the Hudnut administration formulated a plan to build a downtown shopping mall. Other cities were constructing such downtown retail meccas in order to revive their central business districts. Milwaukee opened Grand

Avenue Mall in 1982; St. Louis Centre, with more than 150 stores, welcomed its first shoppers in 1985; and Columbus City Center became the hub of downtown shopping in Ohio's capital in 1989. Indianapolis followed suit with the construction of Circle Centre Mall, located on a once-prime retail site along Washington Street.

Circle Centre was the largest, most complex, and most controversial revitalization project undertaken during the Hudnut era. Advocates of historic preservation protested the destruction of older buildings necessary to make way for the new mall. Financing of the project was a major problem, and the city had to aid the private developers through the issuance of $287 million in bonds. Saks Fifth Avenue and Ayres were the intended anchor stores, but they pulled out of the project, forcing the developers to scramble for substitutes. In 1989 the demolition of existing buildings on the site left a gaping hole in the city's former retail center. This symbol of destruction rather than revitalization stirred further criticism among doubters who viewed the project as a costly mistake. Mayor Hudnut, however, persevered. Later he claimed this was "a critical juncture in the city's history," for "if the mall failed, our national image would be severely tarnished."[12] As ever preoccupied with image and reputation, the mayor could not consider deviating from his preconceived course, which he thought would lead to urban greatness.

Finally, in 1995, Circle Centre opened during the administration of Hudnut's successor, Stephen Goldsmith. Nordstrom and Parisian were the initial anchor stores, and they and an array of specialty shops initially attracted a new generation of shoppers downtown. At the close of the century, Circle Centre seemed a success. The city's ambitious and troubled effort appeared to be paying off.

Mayor Hudnut's final coup involved neither sports nor the city's downtown. In 1989 United Airlines initiated a search for the site of a new maintenance complex that was expected to employ more than six thousand workers. More than ninety cities submitted bids for the facility, offering financial incentives to win the company's favor. Indianapolis assembled a package that United Airlines could not refuse. The state of Indiana would grant the company $15.2 million and issue $159 million in revenue bonds to fund construction of the facility. In addition, the city of Indianapolis would issue $111.5 million in revenue bonds to finance the complex, and the city's airport authority would raise the ante by making improvements to the facility site and issuing additional bonds.

Some observers were outraged by what they deemed an enormous bribe to be paid to a giant corporation. In response, Hudnut asked, "Were we to pass up the opportunity to bring 6,300 jobs into a new $800-million facility that would guarantee an annual payroll of a quarter-billion dollars and indirectly account for 18–20,000 more jobs in this area." The mayor's answer was a resounding no. When he realized that he had succeeded in securing the maintenance facility, Hudnut claimed, "A lump developed in my throat, just as when I walked into the Hoosier Dome with Bob Irsay in early April 1984 to introduce him to the Indianapolis community after he had announced he was moving his NFL team to our city, and some 20,000 people stood up to cheer." At a gathering in November 1991 to celebrate the consummation of the United Airlines deal, the enthusiastic Hudnut proclaimed, "Today is one of the greatest and most exciting days in our city's history."[13] Yet United had only "promised" 6,300 jobs, and according to the old adage, promises were made to be broken. With both Circle Centre Mall and the United Airlines maintenance complex, the city was taking expensive gambles. Taxpayers in future years would need to determine whether the hundreds of millions of dollars invested were paying off.

Yet for the time being, Hudnut could wax emotional about marching into the Hoosier Dome with Irsay and about beating out ninety other cities to secure thousands of United Airlines jobs. When he left office at the close of 1991, he could justifiably claim that he had changed the image of Indianapolis. Observers throughout the nation seemed to believe that Indianapolis had quick-changed into a model city. In 1985 *Newsweek* magazine dubbed Indianapolis "the Cinderella of the Rust Belt," a city that shined in comparison to such dowdy Rust Belt stepsisters as Saint Louis, Detroit, and Cleveland. When Indianapolis secured the United Airlines complex, an Oklahoma City newspaper ran the headline "Can-Do Attitude Credited for Indianapolis Successes." In the wake of the city's United Airlines triumph, a Denver newspaper explained, "This isn't the first time others have underestimated the city that was once known only for auto racing or dismissed as 'the neon cornfield.' Indeed, Indianapolis has established a reputation as an economic development pit bull."[14] A Hartford, Connecticut, newspaper joined in the applause for Indianapolis, claiming it had learned "to aggressively encourage economic growth, to establish a common vision and pursue it with a vengeance." This was a formula that had lifted Indianapolis "out of a tailspin and made it one of the most livable places in America."[15]

As Hudnut had desired, Indianapolis was winning attention and establishing a stellar reputation. It seemed to be a model for urban success and an inspiration for other cities that wanted to reverse decline and achieve new vitality. Mayor Hudnut's cheerleading and boosterish hyperbole had convinced many observers that Indianapolis was truly a showplace and no longer a no place.

Yet the city's soaring reputation veiled some harsh realities. During the Hudnut years, the economic news was not all upbeat. Like other midwestern cities, Indianapolis suffered from the mounting wave of deindustrialization. As factories closed, industrial jobs disappeared, and thousands of workers bore the consequences. Between 1967 and 1987, the number of workers employed in manufacturing in Marion County dropped more than 30 percent, falling from 120,000 to 83,000. Moreover, the decline seemed to be accelerating during the 1980s. In 1983 AT&T announced the closing of the giant Western Electric plant on Indianapolis's east side. As recently as 1979, it had employed 8,100 workers and ranked as the city's sixth-largest employer, only one place behind the fifth-ranked Eli Lilly and Company. For thirty-five years Western Electric had been an economic mainstay and a major presence in the Hoosier capital. Then, in 1987, RCA closed its east-side factory, and Chrysler ended production at its electrical plant across from the defunct RCA facility in 1988. Ten years earlier the Chrysler factory had employed 3,500 workers. In the early 1990s, the Allison Division of General Motors survived as the city's largest manufacturing concern. But even Allison was cutting back, its number of employees dropping from 15,000 in 1979 to 10,400 in 1993. For workers laid off at the shrinking factories, the good news of yet another downtown office tower opening must have provided little solace.

Some of Hudnut's initiatives may have yielded smaller returns than implied by the fanfare and hyperbole issuing from city hall and the chamber of commerce. In 1991 a survey found that the amateur sports organizations and facilities in the city had created only 526 jobs, a small figure compared to the thousands laid off by Western Electric. Despite all the construction in the Mile Square, the share of the Marion County workforce employed downtown actually declined from 30 percent in 1970 to only 21 percent in 1990. From 1983 through 1992, suburban office construction far outpaced office construction downtown. During this decade of downtown revitalization, the central business district recorded 4.14 million square feet of new office space; the suburban figure was 6.58 million square feet. In 1983 occupied downtown office space exceeded that in the suburbs by 223,000 square feet. By 1992, however, the outlying areas led downtown by 1 million square feet. The hard figures indicated that downtown revitalization had not reversed the forces of decentralization. Development along the fringe was still outpacing construction in the urban core.

All the hoopla about sports, office towers, and downtown shopping malls also drew attention away from the most notable generators of jobs in the city. Hospitals and the health-care sector were sources of income for a fast-growing share of Indianapolis residents. Between 1979 and 1993, the number of employees at Methodist Hospital soared 50 percent, from 4,000 to 6,000, and the workforce at St. Vincent Hospital and Health Care Center more than doubled, from 2,300 to 5,700. The education sector was also booming as IUPUI added thousands of new employees at its rapidly expanding campus. Throughout the nation, the so-called Eds-Meds sector was transforming the urban economy as hospitals and educational institutions surpassed shrinking factories and flagging department stores as the dominant employers. Indianapolis was conforming to this emerging pattern. Sports events and glowing press coverage might have boosted the spirits of once-benighted Naptown, but it was the hospitals and the university that were expanding payrolls.

RESTORING THE PAST

As criticism of bulldozing renewal projects mounted in the 1960s and 1970s, urban Americans increasingly came to appreciate the historic built environment threatened by so-called progress. The once-disparaged Victorian past took on new appeal to a public tired of the dismal brutalism of modern concrete structures and the slick glass skins of undistinguished high-rises. A little gingerbread and a few columns with Corinthian capitals brought welcome relief to a generation that had been forced to accept the architectural establishment's rejection of superfluous ornament. Moreover, old neighborhoods of distinguished dwellings and corner shops seemed a desirable alternative to suburbia's subdivisions of cookie-cutter houses and its looming malls surrounded by seas of blacktop. Rather than destroy the past, a growing number of Americans were seeking to preserve it and adapt it to the present.

An increasing number of Indianapolis citizens joined in the emerging movement to preserve the built environment of the past. Beginning in the 1960s, historic preservationists had a marked impact on the Hoosier capital. In the eyes of preservationists, buildings and neighborhoods that had once been condemned as blighted and deserving of demolition became objects of praise, meriting restoration rather than clearing. The result was new life for the structures and districts inherited from earlier years. Historic preservationists thus became key players in the revitalization of Indianapolis. Preservation of the past joined sports and downtown development as a means of reviving the city. Saving the past would supposedly renew the present.

In 1967 the state legislature created the Indianapolis Historic Preservation Commission, with authority to prepare plans for historic districts and control demolition and rehabilitation projects in such districts. However, the commission did not obtain financing and staff support until 1975. From that date onward, it became a significant element in the city's revitalization, adopting plans for neighborhoods and structures designated as historic.

The first neighborhood deemed worthy of preservation was Lockerbie Square, a residential district immediately to the east of downtown. The poet James Whitcomb Riley had lived in the Lockerbie neighborhood, and thus it was sacred ground to the many Indianapolis and Indiana residents who had never shed their reverence for the exalted Hoosier bard. Because of this association, Lockerbie seemed especially deserving of preservation. In 1973 the neighborhood secured listing on the National Register of Historic Places, a federal designation that halted demolition of the district's buildings. Preservation-minded property owners began restoring houses in Lockerbie Square, and the advent of young professionals in the 1970s boosted popular perceptions of the once-declining neighborhood.

Meanwhile, the Old Northside was gradually regaining its reputation as an upscale residential area. During the late nineteenth century, this near-north-side area was the most desirable place to live in the city. Benjamin and Caroline Harrison were its most distinguished residents, but the district also was home to leading merchants H. P. Wasson and L. S. Ayres, as well as Ovid Butler, the founder of the university bearing his name. A home in the neighborhood of Italianate and Queen Anne manses qualified one to a place in the upper echelons of Indianapolis society. It was a neighborhood synonymous with success.

By the 1940s and 1950s, the Old Northside was a prime example of inner-city decline. Many of the large old homes were subdivided into apartments for those who could not afford anything better. Moreover, demolition of aging structures left an increasing number of vacant lots, an unmistakable sign of neighborhood abandonment. In the 1970s, however, some property owners organized to reverse the decline, dedicating themselves to the restoration of the grand old homes. In 1978 the Old Northside was added to the National Register of Historic Places, thereby achieving recognition as a place worth saving. Then, in 1979, the Indianapolis Historic Preservation Commission prepared a preservation plan for the neighborhood, further securing its place on the city's revitalization agenda. Neighborhood residents organized home tours designed to make prospective residents and investors aware of what was being achieved and what could be done in the future to revive the area. Preservationists had to overcome difficulties. In the early 1980s, the Old Northside was known as Indianapolis's premier red-light district. The prevalence of prostitution along the streets once traversed by such Presbyterian worthies as the Harrisons cast a shadow over the district's reputation. In response, the Old Northside Neighborhood Association organized a Prostitution Committee, which effectively cleansed the area of practitioners of the sex trade. By the close of the century, the neighborhood's housing stock had been restored and it was once again a fashionable place to live. Preservation and renovation had brought money back to the inner city.

During the 1980s and 1990s, the fervor for preservation and rehabilitation was spreading to other neighborhoods formerly written off as beyond rejuvenation. On the near north side, the Chatham Arch, St. Joseph, and Herron–Morton Place districts all won recognition from the National Register of Historic Places and were subjects of preservation plans by the city's preservation commission. On the near south side, Fletcher Place and Fountain Square likewise obtained places on the National Register and plans from the city commission. The preservation boom also transformed the near-east-side community of Cottage Home. Unlike the Old Northside, Cottage Home had been a working-class neighborhood of modest frame dwellings in the late nineteenth century. Yet in the late twentieth century, it too was attracting buyers eager to restore the area cottages.

Especially dramatic was the metamorphosis of Massachusetts Avenue. The 1975 survey of Indianapolis architecture had described Massachusetts Avenue as nearly a Skid Row. It was replete with boarded-up storefronts and was a visual testament to inner-city decline. In 1975 there did not seem to be much hope of reversing the avenue's descent. In the 1980s, however, preservationists transformed the street from a slum to an emerging hot spot for investment and renovation. Art galleries, restaurants, law offices, and advertising agencies moved into renovated brick structures that only a decade before had been dismissed as irredeemable. The Massachusetts Avenue of the 1990s demonstrated to once-doubting Hoosiers that historic preservation was an effective strategy for achieving urban revitalization.

The historic preservationists, however, were not only reviving neighborhoods but also restoring prominent buildings from the past. Perhaps the most notable preservation project of the late twentieth century was the restoration of the aging state capitol. By the 1980s it was one hundred years old and showing its age. To commemorate the capitol's centennial anniversary, in 1988 the state completed a thorough renovation of the building aimed primarily at returning the interior to its original appearance. Monumental white oak entrance doors replicating the originals replaced the modern aluminum and glass entries installed in the mid-twentieth century. Interior walls were stripped of the turquoise-blue and sunflower-yellow paint applied in 1958 and were returned to their nineteenth-century appearance. This entailed the recreation of extensive hand-stenciled Victorian designs. Renovators also reproduced the original chandeliers and sconces, replacing the more modern light fixtures that had compromised the Victorian integrity of the building. The dome, which had been leaking, was repaired; columns, capitals, and statuary were thoroughly cleaned; and the original woodwork was repaired and restored. Restoration costs totaled nearly $11 million, more than five times the sum expended for construction of the building in the 1880s. The expense and effort testified to the newfound appreciation of the aesthetics of the age of Benjamin Harrison. Like the rehabilitation of the Old Northside, the restoration of the statehouse clearly announced that Indianapolis's Victorian past was no longer best forgotten.

Indianapolis's iconic Soldiers and Sailors Monument likewise underwent a restoration. The bronze elements of the monument had stained the limestone shaft a greenish color, and some of the candelabrum, decorative railings, and parts of the sculpture and statuary had disappeared over the years. It stood at the very center of the city both geographically and symbolically. Thus, a revitalized Indianapolis required a revitalized monument. The cleansed and restored icon was one more statement declaring that Indianapolis was not sleeping but instead wide awake and ready to assert itself as a rising city.

Another monumental structure from the late nineteenth century that was badly in need of renewal was Union Station. A prime example of Romanesque revival architecture, it had welcomed rail-borne visitors to the city since its opening in the 1880s. With the decline of railroad passenger service, the grand edifice became obsolete, a huge structure serving a dwindling few travelers. By 1980 its survival was in doubt. A massive investment of public and private funds, however, saved it from destruction and transformed it into a much-ballyhooed festival marketplace. Boston and Baltimore had successfully pioneered the festival marketplace concept, and by the 1980s, it was one of the popular panaceas being touted as elixirs for ailing city centers. Basically, it entailed the creation of a fun marketplace of quirky shops and eating places. It was not intended to be a standard mall of chain stores and anchor emporiums. Instead, it was supposed to be an alternative space of food, drink, and retailing, providing an experience one could not find in the suburbs. When it opened in 1986, Union Station festival marketplace conformed to this pattern, with more than one hundred shops and restaurants designed to draw Indianapolis residents and their dollars to the restored relic of the railroad age. It also included a

Central Canal

274-room Holiday Inn that would funnel out-of-town consumers into the marketplace's eating places and retailers. As in the case of Massachusetts Avenue, the Union Station restoration seemed to prove that the past could rejuvenate the present.

A relic of Indianapolis's earlier transportation history also contributed to the city's revitalization. The ill-fated Central Canal, constructed in the 1830s, had survived for the past century and a half, but by the early 1980s, it was a muddy channel littered with trash and bordered by overgrown weeds and brush. It was an eyesore not worthy of Mayor Hudnut's Indianapolis. In the mid-1980s, however, the city launched a $9 million project to convert the canal into an inner-city amenity. A new fountain livened the lower canal basin, and walkways along the banks of the cleansed waterway transformed the downtown liability into an attractive space for residents seeking a respite from nearby city streets. In 1987 Mayor Hudnut presided over a celebration to mark the completion of the first phase of the project. It seemed one more step toward the much-sought-after goal of downtown revitalization. Moreover, it proved that the historic Central Canal, long a reminder of Indianapolis's failure to achieve water access to the world, had finally become a lasting asset to the city.

Meanwhile, Indianapolis preservationists were instilling new life into abandoned industrial buildings. As a growing number of young professionals sought housing in the inner city, investors met that demand by converting old factories into loft apartments. For example, in 1982 the six-story Lockerbie Glove Company factory, constructed in the early twentieth century, was turned into sixty condominiums with twelve-foot ceilings, exposed beams, and unplastered brick walls. Industrial chic was becoming popular in cities across the nation, and Indianapolis did not escape this fashion trend. In 1988 the creation of seventy condominiums in the former Real Silk Hosiery Mills building was another example of the adaptive reuse of manufacturing structures. As in the Lockerbie Glove project, residents of the Real Silk condominiums enjoyed lofty ceilings and ample natural light from the industrial sash windows. Real Silk had been a leading industrial employer in the 1920s and 1930s, but as Indianapolis transitioned from a manufacturing to a service economy, the Real Silk complex found a new purpose—housing white-collar professionals working downtown.

Interest in historic preservation was not confined to the city's white population. By the late 1970s, the traditional hub of African American life around Indiana Avenue seemed doomed to oblivion. With the outward migration of Blacks, the avenue lost its customer base, and racial integration of retail establishments and public accommodations had eliminated the need for a separate Black business district. The expanding IUPUI campus was also eating into the district as housing was bulldozed to make way for the university and medical school. Among the structures threatened with demolition were the apartments of Lockefield Gardens. The model public housing project of the 1930s had deteriorated badly, but Black community leaders and preservationists fought to save it from the wrecking ball. In 1980 a compromise agreement provided that part of the housing project would be leveled but seven of the original buildings would be preserved and restored. It was a partial victory for historical preservationists. At least some of the Black community's historic built environment would survive.

Another project that preserved the city's African American heritage was the restoration of the Madam C. J. Walker Building on Indiana Avenue. Constructed in 1927 as the headquarters of the Walker hair-care business, it also housed a theater comparable to the movie palaces downtown that were frequented by whites. It was, then, a symbol of pride among Indianapolis Blacks. Madam Walker had made a fortune from her business, and her daughter had built this structure as a monument to her mother's success. Moreover, its grand theater proved that Indianapolis Blacks could create an entertainment venue equal to those patronized by whites. It was the city's leading monument to the African American past.

In 1979 the not-for-profit Madam Walker Urban Life Center purchased the building and launched an effort to restore it. The following year the structure was listed on the National Register of Historic Places in recognition that it was a bona fide site worth saving. With private funding, including support from the Lilly Endowment, the fully restored Walker Theatre reopened in 1988.

The wave of preservation revitalizing the inner city entailed human costs as well as benefits. Critics of the so-called gentrification of neighborhoods such as the Old Northside questioned the social justice of displacing poorer residents to make way for upwardly mobile professionals. What was happening to residents priced out of the changing areas? This was a question that troubled some observers. The degree and implications of displacement were debated with no definitive answer. But for those seeking revitalization, the benefits of increased real estate values and rising private investment seemed undeniable. Wealth was a necessary ingredient of urban revival and poverty an indicator of decline. That was the stark truth facing Indianapolis policymakers. Late twentieth-century revitalization was ultimately about attracting and retaining the economic winners.

5

The Twenty-First-Century Metropolis, 2000–2022

In 2000, Indianapolis boasted a population of 782,000 and ranked as the twelfth-largest city in the United States. Unigov's city-county consolidation had given Indianapolis room to grow, and unlike many older cities in the Midwest and Northeast, the Hoosier capital included tracts of undeveloped land available for prospective homeowners. By 2020, Indianapolis's population reached 888,000, boosted in part by two decades of new home construction in outlying areas of the city. Since the adoption of Unigov in 1969, however, city authorities had focused much of their attention on revitalization of the urban core. During the early twenty-first century, this preoccupation with reviving the city center persisted. Some past initiatives proved failures or yielded limited benefits. Other strategies that seemed promising drew continued support from policymakers seeking to enhance the city's fortunes. The coming of the new millennium did not, then, mark a sharp break with the past. Indianapolis continued to grow along its fringes, and the revival of the core was a persistent theme among officials in city hall. Moreover, many of the problems long plaguing the city did not disappear as Indianapolis approached its two-hundredth anniversary in 2020–2021. The early twenty-first century learned from the experiences of the late twentieth century. Yet many of the concerns of the 1980s and 1990s remained troubling preoccupations for city leaders in the 2010s and 2020s.

THE HUDNUT LEGACY AND BEYOND

The energy and enthusiasm of Mayor William Hudnut had left a bold imprint on Indianapolis, and during the early twenty-first century, the city's leaders had to confront his legacy, recognizing its limitations and possibilities. The United Airlines maintenance center was perhaps the most ill-fated initiative of the Hudnut era. In 1991 the mayor had celebrated United Airlines' decision to locate its facility in Indianapolis as one of the greatest achievements in the city's history. The city and state had lured the company to Indianapolis with nearly $300 million of incentives, expecting to benefit handsomely from the estimated 6,300 jobs United Airlines promised to create. In 2003, however, the bankrupt airline closed its Indianapolis facility as part of a downsizing plan intended to cut costs. The maintenance facility had never come close to employing 6,300 Hoosiers, and United had failed to provide the economic boost anticipated a decade earlier. Indianapolis mayor Bart Peterson journeyed to United Airlines' corporate headquarters seeking to convince the company to retain the Indianapolis facility. Yet it was to no avail. Other tenants would occupy the repair base in coming years, but employment levels failed to reach those promised in 1991. Rather than a triumph for the city of Indianapolis, the United Airlines deal was a textbook example of the perils of public incentive financing for economic development.

Another initiative of the late twentieth century that fell far short of expectations was the Union Station project. When the station reopened as a festival marketplace in 1986, it hosted large crowds attracted by the ample publicity celebrating the building's restoration. Yet by the 1990s, the crowds had thinned. Initially, people had come to see what everyone was talking about, but after having viewed the station, they seemed to think there was little reason to return. Many of the eccentric shops sold quirky merchandise that few level-headed Indianapolis shoppers wanted to purchase. There simply was not a profitable market for the goods sold by Candles by Patricia and Al's Wicker Imports. In 1997 the festival marketplace closed, its failure reinforcing fears of downtown doldrums rather than inspiring confidence in rejuvenation. Actually, it was not alone in suffering this fate. Most of the inner-city festival marketplaces that opened in the 1980s were short lived. By the close of the twentieth century, the festival marketplace concept was a proven dud. It was no panacea for downtown decline.

In the twenty-first century, the hotel located in part of the Union Station train shed survived and proved that the much-vaunted project had fostered some commercial success. The hotel leased the grand atrium waiting room for special functions; in 2015 it was the scene of fifty-seven weddings. An assortment of groups also rented office space in the depot. As owner of the space, however, the city was responsible for financing the maintenance and repair of the aging building, and rents did not compensate for this expense. In sum, the Union Station project had not provided the expected boost to the downtown economy, and in the twenty-first century, it was costing the city money. The restoration, however, had saved a structure that deserved salvation. So, the project produced a benefit, but it was a benefit with lingering costs.

The construction of Circle Centre Mall likewise had a mixed legacy. Celebrated as the centerpiece of downtown revival at its opening in 1995, it drew consumer dollars to Washington Street and appeared to prove that Mile Square could still be a shopping destination. The mall continued to prosper during the first decade of the twenty-first century, but it lost one of its anchor stores, the upscale retailer Nordstrom, in 2011. Three years later the offices of the *Indianapolis Star* newspaper moved into the space vacated by Nordstrom, a sign that Circle Centre could no longer survive as solely a retail venue. Then, in 2018, Carson's department store, which had earlier replaced Parisian, closed, leaving Circle Centre without an anchor retailer. In 2020–2021 the shutdowns associated with the COVID-19 pandemic deprived the mall of the convention goers and downtown office workers who constituted its primary customer base. By 2022 Circle Centre's owners were soliciting plans for redeveloping the mall. Despite periodic renovations, Circle Centre was looking tired by the close of the century's second decade. It no longer projected the fresh face of rejuvenation; instead, it presented the sagging countenance of an earlier era when mall shopping was a growing national pastime.

In part, Circle Centre was a victim of changing consumer preferences. As shoppers relied increasingly on online retailing and suburban big-box stores such as Walmart and Target, malls and their department store anchors hemorrhaged business. Indianapolis's suburban malls were failing, joining the expanding ranks of dead malls that littered the fringes of American cities. Indianapolis's first enclosed mall, Lafayette Square, barely survived. For the thousands of motorists who passed Lafayette Square each day on Interstate 65, its long-vacant Ayres store was a decaying monument from the retailing past. Downtown malls in other cities had proved even less viable than Circle Centre. St. Louis Centre closed in 2006, having survived only twenty-one years; Columbus City Center suffered the same fate in 2009, twenty years after its opening. By 2022 Circle Centre had outlasted both, reaching its twenty-seventh birthday. Yet its future as a retail center was in doubt, and no one could seriously claim that it remained a major generator of downtown vitality. Instead, the 1990s symbol of revitalization had become a 2020s problem in search of a solution.

Basically, revival of downtown retailing was no longer a realistic element of the strategy for rejuvenating the urban core. The days of bustling crowds of shoppers converging on Ayres and Block's were past. Shopping patterns had changed, and city policymakers could no longer expect retailing to be the essential tonic for reviving urban centers.

Though both Union Station and Circle Centre seemed to cast doubt on retailing as a major generator of urban revival, the sports strategy so prominent during the Hudnut era continued to be a favored option for boosting Indianapolis's fortunes. Major-league professional sports played in downtown venues had been a key element in the revitalization initiative of the 1980s and would remain a vital part of plans to promote Indianapolis in the early twenty-first century. It proved, however, to be an expensive option. Market Square Arena was demolished in 2001, only twenty-seven years after its opening. The newly constructed Conseco Fieldhouse, which cost $183 million to build, had replaced it as the home of the Indiana Pacers basketball team. Construction of Market Square in the 1970s had cost $23 million. Even adjusting for inflation, the bill for Conseco was more than twice that for Market Square. This increased cost was one of the facts of life that sports-hungry cities faced at the dawn of the twenty-first century. The owners of sports franchises demanded ever more elaborate facilities, and cities needed to accede to their demands to keep their major-league status. The public and private sectors shared the cost of Conseco Fieldhouse, with the public paying $79 million derived from a special professional sports taxing district. In 2010 the Pacers threatened to leave Indianapolis and received additional public funds, which purchased a pledge from the team to remain in the Hoosier capital for at least another nine years.

Retention of the Pacers, however, was a bargain compared with the price tag for keeping the Colts football team. The acquisition of the Colts had been the proudest achievement of the Hudnut era. The professional sports franchise was a symbol of Indianapolis's supposed emergence as a major American city. In the minds of many city leaders, loss of the Colts would be a disaster. A new stadium would keep the team and also improve Indianapolis's chance to host a future Super Bowl, the prize event sought by every ambitious American city in the twenty-first century. Consequently, the city broke ground in 2005 for a new $720 million home for the Colts. To raise the public funds that paid for the bulk of the project, the central Indiana counties surrounding Indianapolis levied a 1 percent food and beverage tax, and Marion County doubled its restaurant sales tax to 2 percent. Marion County also increased its hotel and auto rental tax. When the

Lucas Oil Stadium

newly named Lucas Oil Stadium opened in 2008, the now-obsolete Hoosier Dome was demolished. The once-celebrated stadium that had attracted the Colts in 1984 had survived less than a quarter of a century. At the time of the demolition, the city still had not paid off the debt incurred to construct the Hoosier Dome. By 2008, then, the public sector was committed to paying for both a defunct facility and its costly replacement.

Moreover, the Colts' management benefited handsomely from the deal it negotiated with the city. The Colts agreed to pay only $250,000 annually to play in the new facility and were not responsible for any maintenance costs. In addition, the franchise would receive up to $3.5 million per year from the revenues generated by other events held in the stadium, $6 million annually from naming rights, and the multimillion-dollar profits from stadium concessions. It was a sweet deal for the team owners, who ably took advantage of Indianapolis's insecurity about its status as a big-league city. Indianapolis leaders seemed to believe that loss of the football team would relegate the city to its past existence as minor-league Naptown. To them, it was worth hundreds of millions of dollars to preserve Indianapolis's big-city image.

Some observers criticized Indianapolis's willingness to yield to the Colts' expensive wishes. Economists argued that public subsidies for sports facilities did not pay off, as the economic benefits did not justify the costs. Yet cities throughout the nation were subsidizing sports franchises and offering lucrative deals to attract major-league teams. Intangible benefits such as spirit, image, and prestige, which could not accurately be measured by number-crunching economists, seemed to warrant the subsidies. The prevailing belief among city leaders was that professional sports teams were essential elements of urban vitality.

In 2012 Indianapolis definitely reaped the intangible benefits of image and prestige when it hosted the Super Bowl. With extensive television and press coverage of the stellar event, Indianapolis became a city that could not be ignored or forgotten by millions of American sports fans. For one weekend, it was the center of national attention. It was truly India-SHOW-Place rather than India-NO-Place. Hosting the Super Bowl realized the dreams of Hudnut-era city officials. In the minds of many central Indiana residents, the Super Bowl weekend justified the $720 million spent on the stadium. The sports extravaganza seemed to more than compensate for the 1 or 2 percent added to a restaurant bill.

Despite all the exaltation about the Colts and the Super Bowl, the Indianapolis 500 race remained central Indiana's greatest sporting event and the spectacle that, each year, brought Indianapolis to the attention of the nation as a whole and racing fans throughout the world. In 2000 a study of the economic impact of sport events found that the Indianapolis 500 ranked first in the nation, generating $336.6 million for Indianapolis. In comparison, the Super Bowl held in Atlanta that year had an impact of $215 million.[1] An estimated four hundred thousand spectators attended the Indianapolis event each year, and the one-hundredth running of the race in 2016 proved an especially popular event. As in previous years, the Indianapolis 500 boasted the highest attendance of any single-day sports contest in the world. Moreover, in 1994 the Speedway began hosting the Brickyard 400 NASCAR race, an event that produced an estimated impact of $219.5 million in 2000, again exceeding the Super Bowl. Attendance for the Brickyard 400 dropped in the second decade of the twenty-first century, but the Indianapolis 500 remained an unsurpassed moneymaker. Local leaders feared the loss of the professional football franchise and a possible midnight departure like the one that left Baltimore without a team. The Indianapolis 500, however, was a permanent fixture of the Hoosier scene, having survived for more than a century. Like the Soldiers and Sailors Monument, it was an established icon of the city, and like the monument, it was not going anywhere.

Another generator of income for the local economy was the burgeoning meeting and convention business. The Indianapolis Convention Center, which opened in 1972 and underwent expansions in 1984 and 1993, continued to extend its downtown footprint in the twenty-first century. A 2000–2001 expansion cost $45 million, with two-thirds of the sum coming from the Lilly Endowment. Then, a project completed in 2011 with a $275 million price tag nearly doubled the size of the center. In 2020 the city-county council unanimously approved a bond issue to finance yet another expansion of the facility, with a projected bill of $125 million. This pattern was repeated across the nation as cities vied to attract meetings and conventions by offering ever-improved facilities. Both sports stadiums and convention centers were part of the widely accepted formula for urban revitalization in early twenty-first century America. Just as economists questioned the wisdom of sports subsidies, they doubted whether pouring more money into convention facilities was a

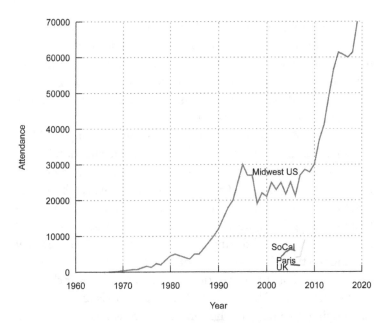

Graph of attendance at the Gen Con game fairs. Note the marked increase in attendance in the years after 2003, when the Midwest-based fair moved from Milwaukee to Indianapolis.

wise investment. Indianapolis leaders, however, thought otherwise. They believed that the expanding downtown meeting venue was a boon to the city and essential to Indianapolis's reputation as a major American city.

Proponents of expansion projects could point to data that seemed to justify their position. The number of major conventions in Indianapolis rose from thirty-five in 1999 to fifty-two in 2019. From 2000 through 2009, the average annual meeting and convention attendance in the city was 340,000; the average annual attendance for 2010–2019 was 494,000. During the first two decades of the century, convention business had generated billions of dollars for the local economy and brought millions of visitors to the city's once-declining downtown. One of the biggest moneymakers was Gen Con, a four-day tabletop game convention held annually in Indianapolis beginning in 2003. The 2011 expansion of the convention center was deemed necessary to accommodate the ever-growing Gen Con. In 2003 Gen Con attracted twenty-five thousand attendees, by 2014 the figure had more than doubled to nearly fifty-seven thousand, and in 2019 it reached a record-setting seventy thousand.

Gen Con and the lesser conventions and meetings held in Indianapolis spelled profits for the city's downtown hotels. The city's skyline reflected the success of the lodging business in Mile Square. During the first decade of the century, the tallest building completed in the city was the twenty-three-story, 287-foot Conrad Indianapolis, a world-class Hilton hotel. The tallest building that opened during the second decade of the century was the thirty-four-story, 376-foot JW Marriott hotel. Plans for the expansion of the convention center in the 2020s included a forty-story Signia Hilton hotel. Less lofty hotels also added to the lodging inventory of the central business district. By 2020 there were approximately 7,800 hotel rooms downtown to accommodate the city's increasing number of visitors.

Whereas the number of high-rise hotels was growing, construction of downtown office towers largely ceased after 1990. During the early twenty-first century, only one office building of more than two hundred feet was constructed in the Mile Square. That was the fourteen-story headquarters of the Simon Property Group, completed in 2006. The Bank One Tower, renamed Salesforce Tower, was Indianapolis's tallest building on completion in 1990, and it remained so three decades later. The early twenty-first century did not witness a repetition of the 1980s boom in high-rise office building construction. This reflected changing economic realities. Downtown remained an office center, and the office sector was not joining the Union Station shops and Circle Centre anchors in the discard bin of downtown development. Yet hospitality, tourism, and the trade generated from visitors were the fastest-growing elements in the continued revitalization of the Mile Square.

The development of White River State Park enhanced downtown Indianapolis's emerging reputation as a magnet for visitors and a center for leisure, tourism, culture, and entertainment. Once a blighted factory district, the park's site was gradually transformed from the late 1980s through the early twenty-first century. In 1988 the Indianapolis Zoo opened on a derelict industrial site. One year later the Eiteljorg Museum of American Indian and Western Art became the park's second attraction. In 1999 a botanical garden welcomed its first visitors, and a year later the National Collegiate Athletic Association Hall of Champions Museum opened to sports fans. The park's largest structure, the $105 million Indiana State Museum, became a stellar attraction when it received its first visitors in 2002. Beginning in 2004, the park presented summer concerts that drew thousands of Indianapolis residents. White River State Park offered a wide range of attractions that lured visitors to downtown Indianapolis. Given the growing number of sports fans, hotel customers, tabletop game players, and zoo and museum visitors converging on downtown in the early twenty-first century, the title "central business district" was increasingly a misnomer for the Mile Square. Downtown Indianapolis was becoming less a place of business and more a place to enjoy oneself and spend one's leisure hours. It was a destination for thousands of people who were taking time off from transacting business.

Upbeat developments on once-depressed Massachusetts Avenue further emphasized the changing nature of the urban core. The button-down-collar, gray-flannel-suited businessman and the hat-and-glove wearing Ayres shopper of the past were alien to the hip scene on Massachusetts Avenue. The avenue's Bottleworks District, which debuted in 2020, was characteristic of the new, fun spirit that was intended to attract dollars to the city's center. The district's centerpiece was the 139-room Bottleworks Hotel located in the former administration building of the Coca-Cola Bottling Plant, an art deco remnant of Indianapolis's industrial past. Also included in the complex was the Garage

Food Hall, with an assortment of eating places that eschewed the bland offerings of the standard suburban mall food court. An eight-screen cinema presented a variety of motion pictures, including the creations of independent filmmakers, and an entertainment center catered to enthusiasts of duckpins, pinball, and craft beers. A second phase of the project included the virtual reality experience SandboxVR, where customers could explore outer space or repel a zombie attack. The district's developer created some office space as well, but this was not to detract from the image of the Bottleworks District as a place of fun and leisure. In the Bottleworks District, one could eat, drink, and enjoy the pleasures of an upscale boutique hotel in a hip environment that seemed to dispel any lingering thoughts of Indianapolis as staid and sleepy.

The Bottleworks District businesses hoped to profit from the growing number of young professionals living downtown. Just as the hotel business was expanding in the Mile Square, so was the inventory of apartments that proved especially attractive to young people seeking places to live close to work and convenient to the eating, drinking, and entertainment venues in the city center. Between 2010 and 2020, the downtown population rose more than 50 percent, increasing from 14,664 to 22,412. During the early twenty-first century, downtown consistently ranked among the fastest-growing residential areas in the city. Older buildings were converted into apartments, and new residential structures opened to accommodate the demand for downtown housing. For example, in 2018 workers completed construction on the twenty-eight-story 360 Market Square building, a $121 million apartment project that included a Starbucks coffee shop and a Whole Foods grocery. It was an upscale residential skyscraper catering to a generation addicted to high-priced lattes and convinced of the merits of organic produce.

Other inner-city areas were also attracting new residents as the incipient gentrification of the 1980s and 1990s accelerated during the first decades of the twenty-first century. Especially notable was the reinvestment in older north-side neighborhoods, which became increasingly white and attracted college-educated newcomers. Aided by massive federal funding, the Fall Creek Place district shed its "Dodge City," violence-ridden reputation and became a sought-after place for white professionals to live. Though half of the new houses in the neighborhood were reserved for buyers with low or moderate incomes, the socioeconomic status of Fall Creek Place rose markedly. Whereas only one-tenth of the residents had bachelor's degrees in 2000, ten years later this figure had climbed to one-half. Average family income more than doubled, and during the second decade of the century, the neighborhood could boast of eateries with such trendy names as Tea's Me, Artisan Picnic, and Shoefly Public House. Moreover, the population went from being predominantly Black to predominantly white.

The same phenomenon was evident in nearby neighborhoods. The Keystone-Monon area went from 54 percent Black in 2010 to 31 percent in 2020 as an influx of young professionals drove up the price of real estate. In the Mapleton–Fall Creek district, African Americans constituted only 2 percent of the population in 1960; by 1983 their share was 87 percent. Yet this figure was down to 67 percent in 2010 and only about 50 percent in 2020. During the second decade of the century, the non-Hispanic white population of the neighborhood rose nearly 45 percent.

On the near east side, the Cottage Home–Holy Cross area underwent a similar transformation as it became wealthier and whiter. Even the south side, long deemed a working-class preserve, was attracting the attention of investors and college-educated home buyers. Fountain Square emerged as a trendy magnet for the young and hip, with pricy restaurants and night spots. Nearby Bates-Hendricks had long housed working-class whites who could not afford the rarefied atmosphere of the north side. By 2020, it too was becoming a target for renovators seeking to flip houses for profit. The television series *Good Bones* made millions of Americans aware of the rehabilitation potential of Bates-Hendricks. This HGTV reality program featured a mother-daughter team who purchased derelict houses in the neighborhood and transformed them for resale. The south side of Indianapolis was winning a reputation as a place experiencing revitalization and deserving investment. In the *Good Bones* series, Indianapolis was literally a showplace. It was restoring itself and winning the attention of television viewers nationwide.

Yet the wave of reinvestment in older neighborhoods heightened concerns about the displacement of poor and minority residents. During the late twentieth century, policymakers had lauded the historic preservation efforts that had supposedly saved older neighborhoods from abandonment and demolition. Some critics had recognized that the downside of preservation was displacement, but few could criticize the Old Northside Neighborhood Association for displacing prostitutes and their pimps. In the early twenty-first century, however, a growing chorus of Black residents rebelled at the prospect of being priced out of their neighborhoods and having to yield their turf to upwardly mobile whites. As in Fall Creek Place, one possible solution was to reserve some housing for low- or moderate-income households. Even then the neighborhood would change as white professionals moved into houses not set aside for the less affluent. Indianapolis was changing as the inner city was again becoming a desirable place to live. But the transformation stirred criticism as well as winning applause.

The census data from 2020 recorded the change in the urban core. During the decade from 2010 to 2020, Center Township gained population for the first time since the 1940s, with the number of residents increasing from 142,787 to 153,549. From 1950 to 2010, the number of residents in Center Township had dropped 58 percent, stark evidence of the outward flow of people to the city's fringes. The 2020 figure, however, was statistical proof that the tide had turned. All the talk about the return to the city was not merely boosterish press palaver. Downtown living was increasing in cities across the nation, and the popularity of programs such as *Good Bones* testified to the widespread interest in rehabilitating old houses. Center Township was growing, and the census returns testified to the long-sought revitalization of Indianapolis's core.

The revitalization of Center Township marked the triumph of revival policies formulated in the Hudnut era. Yet the downtown sports facilities, convention center, hotels, and trendy eating and drinking places were not the principal creators of new jobs in the city. Instead, in 2020 as in 1990, the health-care sector was arguably the leading growth engine in Indianapolis. Never a part of the city's revival strategy, the city's hospitals generated income that sustained thousands of Indianapolis households. In 2020 Indiana University Health employed twenty-three thousand people, Ascension St. Vincent had a workforce of seventeen thousand, and Community Health Network maintained a payroll of eleven thousand employees. Each of these numbers exceeded the employment figure for Eli Lilly, the city's largest manufacturer, as well as the employee count for Walmart, the top-ranked retailer. Moreover, each of the health-care institutions had markedly increased its workforce over the previous decade. Indiana University Health's plans for a new flagship hospital were an even clearer indicator of its significance in the city's economy. With an estimated cost of $1.6 billion, more than twice the price tag for Lucas Oil Stadium, the high-rise structure was expected to prove a major addition to the downtown skyline and a monument to the triumphal role of health care in twenty-first-century Indianapolis.

Health care, neighborhood rehabilitation, conventions, and sports had all been prominent themes of the 1980s and 1990s and continued to play important roles in the development of Indianapolis in the twenty-first century. There was, however, one new development that made the Indianapolis of 2020 a different city from that of 1990. In the twenty-first century, the city's Hispanic population soared, adding a new ethnic dimension in a city long divided along white-Black lines. In 1990 Indianapolis had fewer than 8,000 residents of Hispanic origin, constituting only 1 percent of the population. By 2000 this number had increased to 31,000, or 4 percent of the Indianapolis total. Over the following two decades, the Latino population rose markedly, and by 2020 the number of Hispanics in Indianapolis had risen to 117,000, or 13 percent of the city's residents. This was a relatively small figure compared with the percentages in Florida, Texas, and California cities. But it was a significant demographic change for Indianapolis, which had once boasted of an inordinately small foreign-born population. In the early twenty-first century, Indianapolis, like other American cities, was increasingly more diverse, and it was becoming home to thousands of newcomers from Mexico and Central America.

Another new development of the early twenty-first century was the return of Democrats to power. The consolidation of the city and county under Unigov had ensured Republican victories throughout the late twentieth century. Yet as the Democrat-leaning minority population increased, the LGBTQ community became more prominent, and traditional Republicans migrated to surrounding counties beyond the city limits, Democrats were able to triumph at the polls. Two of the three mayors from 2000 to 2020 were Democrats, and by 2020 only five of the twenty-five members of the city-county council were Republicans. With a supermajority, the Democrats were definitely in control. Democrat policymakers, like their Republican predecessors, remained dedicated to financing the Colts and expanding the convention center. Revitalization of the inner city remained a goal. But at least for Black voters, the partisan change made a difference. African Americans were no longer minority adherents of the minority party. By 2020 they had the advantage of being a force within the ruling political organization.

During the first two decades of the new millennium, the policies inherited from the 1980s and 1990s produced some triumphs and some failures. The United Airlines maintenance center proved largely a bust. Union Station survived, but only wedding guests and those attending other special events enjoyed the grandeur of its former waiting room. Unlike in the heyday of rail passenger service, it was not a public space central to the life of the city. Circle Centre Mall had flourished for a time but was faltering by the new century's second decade. The downtown sports facilities generated civic pride at considerable expense. The convention center brought business to Mile Square, yet it too demanded ever more dollars to feed its appetite for expansion. A residential revival in the inner city brought money back to the urban core; however, it also spawned complaints about displacement of the poor and minorities. Health care continued to provide jobs, and a new foreign-born population added diversity to the city's traditionally bland ethnic picture.

Indianapolis boosters could look back on the century's first two decades with relief. The city was still growing, and its reputation, deemed so important to Hudnut-era policymakers, had not suffered any severe blemishes. It remained a major-league city, a mecca for thousands of tabletop gamers, a destination with an abundance of first-rate hotel rooms, and a metropolis boasting the finest in health care.

THE CHALLENGES

Even the most optimistic twenty-first century booster could not ignore the many challenges that faced Indianapolis and cast a shadow over its seemingly bright future. As in other American central cities, the benefits of revitalization were not distributed evenly across the population. Evidence of decline, distress, and disorder persisted in Indianapolis, as it did in older urban hubs throughout the nation. In Indianapolis and elsewhere, policymakers had to face lingering challenges, some of which seemed insuperable.

One persistent problem was the troubled state of the Indianapolis public schools. The Indianapolis school district served the area that had comprised the city before the Unigov consolidation. In the twenty-first century, the outlying township school districts remained independent and thus escaped some of the ills afflicting the central city district defined by Indianapolis's pre-Unigov boundaries. Moreover, the federal government no longer regarded the townships as necessary participants in any solution to the central school district's problems. Beginning in 1998, busing from the city center to the townships was phased out, and the outward transportation of students ceased altogether in 2016. Henceforth, students living within the boundaries of the Indianapolis Public Schools district had to attend the central city public schools or opt for a private education.

Many concerned parents viewed the public school option as unacceptable. In evaluations of Indiana schools, the Indianapolis district ranked near the bottom, suffering from poor test scores, discipline problems, and unacceptable dropout rates. As perceived problems mounted, enrollments in the Indianapolis district plunged, dropping from 108,000 in 1970 to 49,000 in 1990 to 23,000 in 2020. Though the population of Center Township increased during the second decade of the century, school enrollments continued to decline. The households in gentrified neighborhoods were disproportionately childless. Any children who did live in these increasingly upscale areas were more likely to attend private schools than were youths in the outlying townships.

The Indianapolis district introduced charter schools and magnet schools to stanch the hemorrhaging of students from the system. For example, the excellent Center for Inquiry magnet schools were exceptions to the district's generally dismal record. The student bodies of these magnets, however, were predominantly white, and school board members admitted that the vaunted centers were created to keep affluent whites from abandoning the public schools. Some Black parents protested against what they deemed a reimposition of white educational privilege, something the long experiment with busing had been intended to correct. Some Indianapolis schools performed so poorly that the state intervened and took control of their administration. Yet the state did not remedy the situation. From 2017 through 2019, the Indianapolis Public School district consistently earned a D on the state's annual performance report card. City leaders were grooming the city's image and carefully guarding its reputation, but in the meantime, many of its schools were barely passing. Indianapolis was not a showplace in public education.

Another challenge facing twenty-first-century Indianapolis was the prevalence of poverty. During the second decade of the century, Indianapolis's poverty rate averaged about 20 percent, well above the figure for Indiana and the nation as a whole. A 2020 report sponsored by a major think tank found that the number of high-poverty neighborhoods had increased markedly since 1980. By 2020 one-fourth of the city's neighborhoods fell into the high-poverty category. With the loss of manufacturing jobs in the Shadeland Avenue area, the far east side experienced a rising incidence of economic distress. According to the report, the share of residents falling below the federal government's poverty line in one far east side census tract rose from 12 percent in 1980 to 34 percent in 2018. A disproportionate share of Black neighborhoods fell into the high-poverty category, yet some predominantly white areas also became increasingly poor. In one south-side census tract that was 75 percent non-Hispanic white, the poverty rate climbed from 11 percent to 35 percent between 1980 and 2018.[2]

During the early twenty-first century, poverty was spreading more rapidly than gentrification in purportedly revitalized Indianapolis. The media and chamber of commerce boosters might focus on reinvestment in inner-city neighborhoods and the return of affluent home buyers to the urban core, but the proliferation of poverty was inescapable to objective observers. Compared to the nation and the state, Indianapolis was disproportionately poor, and many of its neighborhoods were experiencing unabated economic decline. Thousands of Indianapolis residents did not share fully in the city's good life. They could not afford Colts season tickets, weekend stays at the boutique Bottleworks Hotel, or a wedding at Union Station.

The persistence of the homeless population further testified to the degree of distress in the city. During the 2010s the city conducted an annual count of the homeless and found that about

1,600 Indianapolis residents fell within this category. Visitors to downtown Indianapolis might think this was an undercount, as it was difficult not to notice the distressed individuals napping on the park benches of the War Memorial Plaza or crouching on the sidewalks not far from Monument Circle. They were living evidence that the sports and downtown development strategies had not rid the city of its problems. Fortunately for reputation-conscious city leaders, skywalks connected the leading hotels to the convention center so out-of-town attendees could proceed to their meetings without being exposed to the homeless on the street below.

A persistent challenge for Indianapolis policymakers was the state of race relations in the city. Throughout its history, the city had coped with the divide separating Blacks and whites. In the late nineteenth and early twentieth centuries, a pattern of racial segregation had prevailed, assigning the two races to separate turfs and mandating a subordinate status for African Americans. In the mid- and late twentieth century, the courts and legislators outlawed de jure segregation, yet racial tensions persisted. Most notably, the relations between African Americans and the police remained tense, and in the early twenty-first century, this tension did not disappear.

This was evident on the weekend of May 29–30, 2020, when Indianapolis experienced the worst race-related unrest in its history. In cities across the nation, there were demonstrations to protest the killing of George Floyd, an African American, by a police officer in Minneapolis. African Americans in Indianapolis were also angry about the police shooting of a young Black man, Dreasjon Reed, earlier in the month. The Indianapolis protesters gathered at Monument Circle on the evening of Friday, May 29. Originally peaceful, the protesters became more aggressive and, according to the police, began throwing projectiles at the officers monitoring the situation. The police responded with chemical spray, and the demonstration spiraled into a full-scale riot. On both Friday and Saturday nights, the very heart of the city was the scene of gunfire, looting, and destruction. Rioters smashed the windows of downtown stores and banks, looters invaded Circle Centre Mall, and a fire destroyed a CVS Pharmacy. In the building that had formerly housed Block's, the T. J. Maxx store was also the scene of looting and arson. According to the police, the rioting resulted in two deaths, 174 arrests, and $7 million in financial losses. Moreover, it exacerbated the rift between the police and the African American community. Racial harmony remained a challenge for the city and as yet an elusive goal.

For central Indiana residents who sought to escape from the racial conflict, homelessness, impoverished neighborhoods, and troubled schools of Indianapolis, the fast-growing counties surrounding the city offered an alternative lifestyle and posed a challenge to the city's continued growth and prosperity. During the early twenty-first century, these fringe counties were emerging as potential rivals and competitors, threatening to drain Indianapolis of relatively affluent taxpayers and businesses that could generate much-needed tax dollars. Between 2000 and 2020, the population of Hendricks County to the west rose 70 percent from 104,000 to 175,000; to the south, Johnson County's population increased about 40 percent, as did the number of residents in Hancock County to the east.

Yet the most dramatic growth was to the north, where Hamilton County's population almost doubled, reaching 347,000 in 2020. Money continued to migrate northward, as it had since the mid-nineteenth century, meaning that Hamilton County captured a growing share of the wealth in central Indiana. As Indianapolis added an ever-larger number of impoverished neighborhoods, Hamilton County attracted affluent home buyers and lured businesses seeking well-educated, white-collar employees. Indicative of the change was the census bureau's relabeling of metropolitan Indianapolis as the Indianapolis-Carmel-Anderson metropolitan area. By 2020, Carmel, the largest Hamilton County city, was regarded as one of the anchor cities of the central Indiana metropolitan area. No longer did the census bureau regard the metropolitan agglomeration as focused on the single center of Indianapolis. Instead, the expanding metropolitan area had multiple nuclei, one of which was booming Carmel.

As late as 1960, Carmel had only fourteen hundred residents, but by 2020 its population had climbed to nearly one hundred thousand. During the early twenty-first century, under Mayor Jim Brainard, Carmel developed its own urban-style downtown, complete with a performing arts center that resembled a grand European opera house, a luxury boutique hotel, and a walkable arts and design district with a variety of shops to satisfy the most avid consumer. Its Meridian Street corridor claimed to have the second-largest concentration of office workers in Indiana. More than 125 corporations had their headquarters in the flourishing Hamilton County community. Carmel's residents were well-to-do and well educated; its poverty rate was only 4 percent, one-fifth that of Indianapolis. The schools were excellent, no homeless people hung around Carmel's city center, and rioters were not smashing windows in Mayor Brainard's domain. It seemed to have the advantages of a city as well as those of an affluent suburb. It was not a bland collection of suburban subdivisions. Instead, it had urban pretensions without urban problems. As such, it posed a potent challenge to the older, and somewhat distressed, hub of Indianapolis.

In addition, Carmel's success garnered the laudatory national attention that Mayor Hudnut had always craved. In 2020 *Newsweek* named it the "Best Place to Live in the Midwest," and in 2018 *Niche* ranked it as the "Best Place to Live in America" and *Money* rated it the number three "Best Place to Live in America." It seemed to be an ideal community, located just beyond the boundary of a still-troubled Indianapolis.

Other communities north of Indianapolis were also attracting residents and businesses. Immediately to the north of Carmel, the city of Fishers was home to nearly one hundred thousand people in 2020 and was developing the Nickel Plate District, its own version of an urban-style downtown similar to that created in Carmel. The fastest-growing communities, however, were in southeastern Boone County, where Zionsville and Whitestown were emerging as favorites of central Indiana home buyers with enough money to afford them. Between 2000 and 2020, Zionsville's population soared from nine thousand to thirty-one thousand, and in the 2010s, Whitestown consistently ranked as Indiana's most rapidly growing municipality. In 2000 it was home to fewer than five hundred residents; by 2020 this number had risen to more than ten thousand.

Indianapolis continued to grow and was not built up. Many Hoosiers were attracted to the vibrancy of its urban core. Yet the older city faced the challenge of newer outlying communities that lured residents at a rapid rate and offered an alternative to the central city for businesses seeking to relocate. In 1944 the Committee for Postwar Planning had warned of decentralization and the threat it posed to Indianapolis's growth and prosperity. Unigov had allayed the adverse consequences of outward migration, but by 2020 policymakers had to face the prospect of competition from communities beyond Marion County. In the 2020s, as in the 1940s, decentralization posed a possibly daunting challenge for Indianapolis. Unigov had granted a temporary reprieve, but not a permanent halt, to the diffusion of metropolitan authority.

TWO HUNDRED YEARS

In 2020–2021 Indianapolis celebrated the two-hundredth anniversary of its founding. In 2018 Mayor Joe Hogsett appointed a bicentennial commission to plan anniversary events and programs. Among the initiatives were a bicentennial logo contest and the creation of a series of murals depicting legendary Indianapolis figures. For example, a mural at Indianapolis International Airport celebrated Madam C. J. Walker. The Indiana Historical Society presented an exhibit focusing on the city's centennial pageant of 1920, and the bicentennial commission distributed materials to elementary school students that taught them about the origins of Indianapolis. For older celebrants, a local brewery created a special "Indy Turns 200" beer, which sold for $12.50 a can, and a local distillery introduced a commemorative bicentennial bourbon.

The city's two hundred years of history deserved this range of celebratory events and libations. By 2020–2021 Indianapolis residents could look back on a distinctive past that in some ways distinguished their hometown from similar-sized communities. From its very beginnings, Indianapolis was a place apart. Unlike the overwhelming majority of American cities, Indianapolis was the creation of public enterprise. Private developers seeking a profit did not lay out the frontier village of the 1820s. Instead, the state owned the original town site and named it. State employees surveyed the plat and named the streets. And the state sold the lots to fund the construction of public buildings. In later years, many Indianapolis leaders would fervently espouse private enterprise and oppose public sector interference. The public sector, however, laid the foundations of the capital city.

Unlike most successful nineteenth-century American cities, Indianapolis was not located on a reliably navigable body of water. The leading American cities were seaports or distribution centers on major navigable rivers or lakes. Early Indianapolis promoters despaired of their landlocked locale, which seemed to doom the town to an unpromising future. Perhaps no American city benefited from the advent of the railroad more than Indianapolis. Boosters in the second half of the nineteenth century justifiably called Indianapolis "the Railroad City." Other cities had rail links equal to those of Indianapolis, but no other emerging American hub was so dependent on the railroad for its growth and prosperity. The railroad liberated Indianapolis from its dreary isolation and made it a major city.

Like other major northern cities, Indianapolis attracted European immigrants, most notably Germans. Such German families as the Vonneguts, Liebers, and Frenzels were prominent in the city's development. Yet Indianapolis did not have as rich an immigrant heritage as other major cities in the northern United States. By the turn of the twentieth century, Indianapolis promoters were boasting of the city's overwhelmingly native-born American population. It was, then, fertile ground for the nativist Ku Klux Klan in the 1920s. Indianapolis was more purely American than its northern peers and thus freer of the supposedly pernicious foreign influences that the Klan deplored.

Indianapolis was not, however, purely white. In the late nineteenth century, the African American share of the population was unusually high for a northern city. The Great Migration of Blacks from the South in the early twentieth century increased the number of African Americans in Indianapolis, but the impact was not as marked as in many other northern cities, where the original established Black community had constituted a smaller portion of the white population. Otherwise, Indianapolis did not differ from the American norm for race relations. The Hoosier capital was not immune from the racial tensions commonplace in urban America. In the twentieth and twenty-first centuries, Indianapolis, like its peers, suffered from a legacy of distrust and division.

During the late nineteenth and early twentieth centuries, Indianapolis's monumental war memorials further distinguished the city from similar-sized cities elsewhere in the nation. With its soaring tower, abundant statuary, and cascading fountains, the Soldiers and Sailors Monument was a flamboyant centerpiece for the city. It was an exuberant exclamation point at the very heart of the city that announced to onlookers that Indianapolis, like the Apostle Paul's Tarsus, was no mean city but instead a significant place that deserved respect and attention. It was an urban icon, and Monument Circle was an urban space few American cities could match. The War Memorial Plaza further distinguished the city as a showplace of monumental patriotism. The memorial building was patterned after one of the seven wonders of the ancient world, although the Indianapolis version was bigger. Indianapolis thus surpassed the grandeur and glory of antiquity. With its grand monumental spaces, downtown Indianapolis was something more than simply a typical American central business district with office buildings, hotels, and department stores. Its unsurpassed monuments set it apart from run-of-the mill midwestern commercial centers.

Another distinguishing feature of twentieth-century Indianapolis was the Indianapolis 500 race. With the exception of Louisville, home of the Kentucky Derby, no other major American city hosted a single sporting event that placed it in the limelight each year. The Super Bowl and World Series were sports spectacles that a fortunate city might secure once in a decade. Twenty-nine other cities could boast of a major-league football team vying with the Colts for attention, but there was only one city that was home to the greatest spectacle in auto racing. Each Memorial Day weekend, Indianapolis was the focus of attention of millions of race fans and the destination for hundreds of thousands of visitors filling the tills of area restaurants and paying inflated rates for hotel rooms. At the close of May each year, Indianapolis was in the forefront of American consciousness.

Unigov was Indianapolis's most distinguishing characteristic of the late twentieth century and perhaps its greatest achievement of the years since World War II. The city severed the suburban noose that strangled many older American central cities that consequently suffered declining populations, shrinking tax rolls, and what some perceived as permanent disability. The consolidated city and county of Indianapolis continued to grow, and it enjoyed a solid financial base. It was not another Cincinnati, Cleveland, or Saint Louis. Rather, Indianapolis had done what few others were able to achieve. It had overcome, at least for the following half century, the worst effects of decentralization.

In 2020–2021, then, Indianapolis residents had good reason to celebrate their city's past. It was indeed no mean city; it was a place with a significant history that set it apart as worthy of consideration and some applause. Some observers might dismiss Indianapolis's past as undramatic. It did not suffer a great fire like Chicago or a devastating earthquake like San Francisco. Unlike Atlanta, it was not the scene of Civil War combat, and it did not endure a national-anthem-inspiring siege as Baltimore did during the War of 1812. Indianapolis's history was relatively placid and devoid of disasters. Its only president was Benjamin Harrison, a figure who has elicited more yawns than plaudits. Yet Indianapolis overcame its early disabilities and rose in the nation's urban ranks. It has a distinctive history of many successes and some failures and faces a future that is both promising and problematic.

NOTES

1. A STATE CAPITAL IS BORN, 1820–1850

1. Donald F. Carmony, *Indiana, 1816–1850: The Pioneer Era* (Indianapolis: Indiana Historical Bureau and Indiana Historical Society, 1998), 108.

2. W. R. Holloway, *Indianapolis: A Historical and Statistical Sketch of the Railroad City* (Indianapolis: Indianapolis Journal Press, 1870), 10.

3. Jacob Piatt Dunn, *Greater Indianapolis: The History, the Industries, the Institutions, and the People of a City of Homes* (Chicago: Lewis, 1910), 1:27.

4. Ernestine Bradford Rose, *The Circle: "The Center of Our Universe"* (Indianapolis: Indiana Historical Society, 1957), 357.

5. Dunn, *Greater Indianapolis*, 1:72.

6. Dunn, 1:84–85.

7. Dunn, 1:75.

8. Dunn, 1:80.

9. John Scott, *The Indiana Gazetteer or Topographical Dictionary* (Centreville, IN: John Scott and William Doughty, 1826), 70.

10. Dunn, *Greater Indianapolis*, 1:93.

11. Rose, *The Circle*, 363.

12. Carmony, *Indiana*, 142.

13. Carmony, 143.

14. Dunn, *Greater Indianapolis*, 1:18–19.

15. Pamela J. Bennett and Shirley S. McCord, comps., *Progress after Statehood: A Book of Readings* (Indianapolis: Indiana Historical Bureau, 1974), 151.

16. Holloway, *Indianapolis*, 33.

17. Holloway, 33.

18. *A. C. Howard's Directory, for the City of Indianapolis* (Indianapolis: A. C. Howard, 1857), 35.

19. Holloway, *Indianapolis*, 42–43.

20. Berry R. Sulgrove, *History of Indianapolis and Marion County, Indiana* (Philadelphia: L. H. Everts, 1884), 104.

21. Sulgrove, *History of Indianapolis*, 104.

22. *Howard's Directory*, 35.

23. Holloway, *Indianapolis*, 43.

24. Howard's Directory, 36.

25. Holloway, *Indianapolis*, 36; Henry Ward Beecher, *Lectures to Young Men, on Various Important Subjects* (New York: Saxton & Miles, 1846).

26. William C. Beecher and Rev. Samuel Scoville, *A Biography of Rev. Henry Ward Beecher* (New York: Charles L. Webster, 1888), 206.

27. Emma Bullard Beecher, *From Dawn to Daylight; or, the Simple Story of a Western Home* (New York: Derby & Jackson, 1860), 140.

28. *Howard's Directory*, 43.

29. Holloway, *Indianapolis*, 85.

30. Dunn, *Greater Indianapolis*, 1:148–149.

31. Dunn, 1:148.

32. Bennett and McCord, *Progress After Statehood*, 152–153.

33. Holloway, *Indianapolis*, 83.

34. *Indianapolis of To-Day* (Indianapolis: Consolidated Illustrating, 1896), 32.

35. Holloway, *Indianapolis*, 90.

36. John H. B. Nowland, *Early Reminiscences of Indianapolis* (Indianapolis: Sentinel Book and Job Printing House, 1870), 102.

2. INDIANAPOLIS TAKES OFF, 1850–1900

1. Jacob Piatt Dunn, *Greater Indianapolis: The History, the Industries, the Institutions, and the People of a City of Homes* (Chicago: Lewis, 1910), 1:434.

2. Dunn, *Greater Indianapolis*, 1:435.

3. *Indianapolis of To-Day* (Indianapolis: Consolidated Illustrating, 1896), 68.

4. Dunn, *Greater Indianapolis*, 1:322.

5. Dunn, 1:329.

6. *Indianapolis of To-Day*, 72.

7. Jerry Marlette, *Indianapolis Railways: A Complete History of the Company and Its Predecessors from 1864 to 1957* (Terra Alta, WV: Pioneer Press of West Virginia, 2002), 3.

8. Marlette, *Indianapolis Railways*, 29.

9. Dunn, *Greater Indianapolis*, 1:423.

10. Dunn, 1:105.

11. Berry R. Sulgrove, *History of Indianapolis and Marion County, Indiana* (Philadelphia: L. H. Everts, 1884), 253.

12. Oliver H. Smith, *Early Indianapolis Trials and Sketches* (Cincinnati: Moore, Wilstach, Keys, 1858), 286.

13. Smith, *Early Indiana Trials*, 424.

14. *G. W. Hawes' Indiana State Gazetteer and Business Directory, for 1858 and 1859* (Indianapolis: George W. Hawes, 1858), 1:128.

15. Wylie J. Daniels, *The Village at the End of the Road* (Indianapolis: Indiana Historical Society, 1933), 101.

16. Shirley S. McCord, comp., *Travel Accounts of Indiana 1679–1961* (Indianapolis: Indiana Historical Bureau, 1970), 216.

17. Sulgrove, *History of Indianapolis*, 445–446.

18. Max R. Hyman, ed., *The Journal Handbook of Indianapolis* (Indianapolis: Indianapolis Journal Newspaper, 1902), 338.

19. Libby Cierzniak, "Indianapolis Collected: Miracle on Washington Street," HistoricIndianapolis.com, December 24, 2011, https://historicindianapolis.com/indianapolis-collected-miracle-on -washington-street/.

20. Kenneth L. Turchi, *L. S. Ayres & Company: The Store at the Crossroads of America* (Indianapolis: Indiana Historical Society, 2012), 10.

21. Turchi, *L. S. Ayres*, 13.

22. *Fourth Biennial Report of the Department of Statistics for 1891–92* (Indianapolis: William B. Burford, 1892), 28–29.

23. Marlette, *Indianapolis Railways*, 33.

24. Eva Draegert, "Cultural History of Indianapolis: Music, 1875–1890," *Indiana Magazine of History* 53, no. 3 (September 1957): 265.

25. George Theodore Probst, *The Germans in Indianapolis 1840–1918* (Indianapolis: German-American Society and Indiana German Heritage Society, 1989), 66.

26. Judith E. Endelman, *The Jewish Community of Indianapolis, 1849 to the Present* (Bloomington: Indiana University Press, 1984), 57.

27. Dunn, *Greater Indianapolis*, 1:252.

28. Dunn, 1:253.

29. W. R. Holloway, *Indianapolis: A Historical and Statistical Sketch of the Railroad City* (Indianapolis: Indianapolis Journal Press, 1870), 165.

30. Dunn, *Greater Indianapolis*, 1:273.

31. Herman Murray Riley, "A History of Negro Elementary Education in Indianapolis," *Indiana Magazine of History* 26, no. 4 (December 1930): 292–293.

32. Dunn, *Greater Indianapolis*, 1:131; *Hawes' Indiana State Gazetteer*, 1:129.

33. *The First Annual Report of the Public Library of Indianapolis 1873–4* (Indianapolis: Printing and Publishing House, 1874), 17.

34. *First Annual Report of the Public Library*, 17.

35. Eva Draegert, "Cultural History of Indianapolis Literature, 1875–1890," *Indiana Magazine of History* 52, no. 3 (September 1956): 225.

36. Jean Snoddy, "Fortnightly History at 100 Years," Fortnightly Literary Club, October 1985, https://fortnightly.org/history/.

37. Ann Mauger Colbert, "Propylaeum," in *The Encyclopedia of Indianapolis*, ed. David J. Bodenhamer and Robert G. Barrows (Bloomington: Indiana University Press, 1994), 1137.

38. Anne P. Robinson and S. L. Berry, *Every Way Possible: 125 Years of the Indianapolis Museum of Art* (Indianapolis: Indianapolis Museum of Art, 2008), 32.

39. Harriet G. Warkel, "A Magazine 'Perilously Fine': Joseph Moore Bowles and *Modern Art*," *Traces of Indiana and Midwestern History* 6, no. 1 (Winter 1994): 9.

40. Robert M. Taylor and Barry Shifman, "The Arts and Crafts Movement in Indianapolis," *Traces of Indiana and Midwestern History* 6, no. 1 (Winter 1994): 6.

41. Wilhelmina Seegmiller, "The Arts and Crafts Movement in Indianapolis," *Brush and Pencil* 4, no. 4 (July 1899): 213.

42. Benjamin Harrison, "No Mean City," in *After Dinner Speeches and How to Make Them*, ed. William Allen Wood (Chicago: T. H. Flood, 1914), 90.

3. REACHING MATURITY, 1900–1945

1. *Annual Report of Public Service Commission of Indianapolis for the Fiscal Year Ending September 30, 1914* (Indianapolis: William B. Burford, 1914), 26.

2. Sigur E. Whitney, *The Indianapolis Automobile Industry: A History, 1893–1939* (Jefferson, NC: McFarland, 2018), 94.

3. Jerry M. Fisher, *The Pacesetter: The Untold Story of Carl G. Fisher* (Fort Bragg, CA: Lost Coast Press, 1998), 42.

4. Charles Leerhsen, *Blood and Smoke: A True Tale of Mystery, Mayhem, and the Birth of the Indy 500* (New York: Simon & Schuster, 2011), 144, 146–147.

5. Ralph Kramer, *Indianapolis Motor Speedway: 100 Years of Racing* (Iola, WI: Krause, 2009), 52; Leerhsen, *Blood and Smoke*, 197.

6. Leerhsen, 196.

7. Ophelia Georgiev Roop and Lilia Georgiev Judson, "Bulgarians/Macedonians," in *Peopling Indiana: The Ethnic Experience*, ed. Robert Taylor Jr. and Connie McBirney (Indianapolis: Indiana Historical Society, 1996), 539.

8. Paul J. Ramsey, "The War against German-American Culture: The Removal of German Language Instruction from the Indianapolis Schools, 1917–1919," *Indiana Magazine of History* 98, no. 4 (December 2002): 298.

9. *Indianapolis Turnverein: Seventy-Fifth Anniversary 1851–1926* (Indianapolis: Indianapolis Turnverein, 1926), 21.

10. Kurt Vonnegut Jr., *Palm Sunday: An Autobiographical Collage* (New York: Delacorte, 1981), 21.

11. Ray Stannard Baker, *Following the Color Line: An Account of Negro Citizenship in the American Democracy* (New York: Doubleday, Page, 1908), 124.

12. Baker, *Following the Color Line*, 117–118.

13. Jacob Piatt Dunn, *Greater Indianapolis: The History, the Industries, the Institutions, and the People of a City of Homes* (Chicago: Lewis, 1910), 1:253.

14. Emma Lou Thornbrough, "Segregation in Indiana during the Klan Era of the 1920's," *Mississippi Valley Historical Review* 47, no. 4 (March 1961): 603.

15. Thornbrough, "Segregation in Indiana," 603–604.

16. Thornbrough, 598.

17. Thornbrough, 598–599.

18. John Barlow Martin, "The Rise and Fall of D.C. Stephenson," in *The Hoosier State: Readings in Indiana History, the Modern Era*, ed. Ralph D. Gray (Grand Rapids, MI: William B. Eerdmans, 1980), 254.

19. Kenneth L. Turchi, *L. S. Ayres & Company: The Store at the Crossroads of America* (Indianapolis: Indiana Historical Society, 2012), 19–20.

20. "Opening of the Wm. H. Block Company's New Store," *Indianapolis Star*, October 3, 1911, 11.

21. Max R. Hyman, ed., *Hyman's Handbook of Indianapolis* (Indianapolis: M. R. Hyman, 1907), 274.

22. James H. Madison, *Eli Lilly: A Life, 1885–1977* (Indianapolis: Indiana Historical Society, 1989), 62; E. J. Kahn Jr., *All in a Century: The First 100 Years of Eli Lilly and Company* (Indianapolis: Eli Lilly and Company, 1976), 100–101.

23. Turchi, *L. S. Ayres*, 77.

24. Indianapolis Post-War Planning Committee, *Post-War Plans for Indianapolis* (Indianapolis: Indianapolis Chamber of Commerce, 1944), 3, 12.

25. Indianapolis Post-War Planning Committee, *Post-War Plans*, 12–13.

4. EXPANSION AND RENEWAL, 1945–2000

1. Kenneth L. Turchi, *L. S. Ayres & Company: The Store at the Crossroads of America* (Indianapolis: Indiana Historical Society, 2012), 183.

2. Turchi, *L. S. Ayres*, 185.

3. Turchi, 187.

4. *Indianapolis Architecture* (Indianapolis: Indiana Architectural Foundation, 1975), 37, 51.

5. Emma Lou Thornbrough, "Breaking Racial Barriers to Public Accommodations in Indiana, 1935 to 1963," *Indiana Magazine of History* 83, no. 4 (November 1987): 320.

6. Paul Mullins, "Suburbanization and the Color Line along Grandview Drive," *Invisible Indianapolis* (blog), June 29, 2017, https://invisibleindianapolis.wordpress.com/2017/06/29/suburbanization-and-the-color-line-along-grandview-drive/.

7. Emma Lou Thornbrough, *Indiana Blacks in the Twentieth Century* (Bloomington: Indiana University Press, 2000), 178.

8. "Negroes Oppose Lugar Unigov Plan," *Indianapolis Recorder*, January 25, 1969, 1.

9. Thornbrough, *Indiana Blacks*, 184–185.

10. Michael Tackett, "Black Youth's Death Stirs Indianapolis Tension," *Chicago Tribune*, October 2, 1987, https://www.chicagotribune.com/news/ct-xpm-1987-10-02-8703140683-story.html.

11. William H. Hudnut III, *The Hudnut Years in Indianapolis, 1976–1991* (Bloomington: Indiana University Press, 1995), 22–23.

12. Hudnut, *Hudnut Years*, 90.

13. Hudnut, 115, 120, 121.

14. Hudnut, 5.

15. Hudnut, 122.

5. THE TWENTY-FIRST-CENTURY METROPOLIS, 2000–2022

1. Peter McLaren, "Indy Too Leads US Events in Economic Impact," Crash, April 12, 2001, https://www.crash.net/indycar/news/12619/1/indy-500-leads-us-events-in-economic-impact; Joe Drape, "Indy 500: Bigger than the Super Bowl," Fiscal Times, May 27, 2010, https://www.thefiscaltimes.com/Articles/2010/05/27/INDY-500-Bigger-than-the-Superbowl-Eat-Your-Heart-Out-NY.

2. August Benzow and Kenan Fikri, *The Persistence of Neighborhood Poverty* (Washington, DC: Economic Innovation Group, 2020), 25–26.

FURTHER READING

Encyclopedia of Indianapolis, n.d. https://indyencyclopedia.org.

Endelman, Judith E. *The Jewish Community of Indianapolis, 1849 to the Present*. Bloomington: Indiana University Press, 1989.

Hudnut, William. *The Hudnut Years in Indianapolis, 1976–1991*. Bloomington: Indiana University Press, 1995.

Leary, Edward A. *Indianapolis: The Story of a City*. Indianapolis: Bobbs-Merrill, 1971.

Madison, James H. *Eli Lilly: A Life, 1885–1977*. Indianapolis: Indiana Historical Society, 1989.

Probst, George Theodore. *The Germans in Indianapolis 1840–1918*. Indianapolis: German American Society and Indiana German Heritage Society, 1989.

Robinson, Anne P., and S. L. Berry. *Every Way Possible: 125 Years of the Indianapolis Museum of Art*. Indianapolis: Indianapolis Museum of Art, 2008.

Turchi, Kenneth L. *L. S. Ayres & Company, The Store at the Crossroads of America*. Indianapolis: Indiana Historical Society, 2012.

Williams, David Leander. *African Americans in Indianapolis: The Story of a People Determined to Be Free*. Bloomington: Indiana University Press, 2022.

INDEX

Jon C. Teaford is Professor of History at Purdue University. He is author of a number of books on American urban history, including *City and Suburb: The Political Fragmentation of Metropolitan America, 1850–1970* and *The Rough Road to Renaissance: Urban Revitalization in America, 1940–1985*.

For Indiana University Press

Tony Brewer *Artist and Book Designer*
Dan Crissman *Trade and Regional Acquisitions Editor*
Emma Getz *Editorial Assistant*
Samantha Heffner *Marketing and Publicity Manager*
Brenna Hosman *Production Coordinator*
Katie Huggins *Production Manager*
David Miller *Lead Project Manager/Editor*
Dan Pyle *Online Publishing Manager*
Pamela Rude *Senior Artist and Book Designer*